Shortly after coming to faith, I was introd
through The Navigators' Topical Memory System. This launched me on
a passionate pursuit to continuously hide God's Word in my heart. Years
later, I heard Michael Frost expound on the BELLS habits for living on
mission (explained in his book *Surprise the World*). I love that *Hide This
in Your Heart* combines the life-altering missional engagement of BELLS
with the equally life-changing power of Scripture memory. Those
who combine the discipline of Scripture memory with the practice
of radically loving people will be deeply blessed—and will become a
profound blessing to the people in their world.

    AL ENGLER, mission director, The Navigators

What a timely book for us, as followers of Jesus, in this current
landscape. So often memorizing Scripture and getting on mission are
seen as opposed disciplines. However, the longer I join God at work and
follow in his Son's footsteps, the more I realize that I need good rhythms
in my life and that my own disciplines of prayer and reading are tied up
in my understanding of God and his Kingdom. This book is a fantastic
practical read for anyone wanting to grow healthy rhythms and fall
in love with Scripture in fresh ways. I highly recommend it from two
friends and colleagues whose lives have been lived out in these pages.

    KIM HAMMOND, lead pastor, CityLife Church in Casey, Australia; coauthor
of *Sentness: Six Postures of Missional Christians*

What a wonderful pairing of Frost and Hill, showing us how to ground
our lives in the meditations, mantras, and truths of the Bible. To
memorize Scripture is to be formed by the wisdom of God in Christ for
the love of the world. This book is an essential guide for our time.

    CHRISTIANA RICE, codirector, Parish Collective; coauthor of *To Alter Your
World: Partnering with God to Rebirth Our Communities*

MEMORIZING
SCRIPTURE
FOR KINGDOM IMPACT

hide this
in your heart

MICHAEL FROST &
GRAHAM JOSEPH HILL

*A NavPress resource published in alliance
with Tyndale House Publishers*

NavPress is the publishing ministry of The Navigators, an international Christian organization and leader in personal spiritual development. NavPress is committed to helping people grow spiritually and enjoy lives of meaning and hope through personal and group resources that are biblically rooted, culturally relevant, and highly practical.

For more information, visit NavPress.com.

The Team:
Don Pape, Publisher; David Zimmerman, Acquisitions Editor; Leanne Rolland, Copy Editor; Jennifer Phelps, Designer

Cover photograph of folded paper copyright © Katsumi Murouchi/Getty Images. All rights reserved. Origami heart by Elijah Chen, photograph copyright © Tyndale House Publishers. All rights reserved.

Author photograph of Graham Hill and Michael Frost copyright © 2019 by Grace Hill and used with permission.

For information about special discounts for bulk purchases, please contact Tyndale House Publishers at csresponse@tyndale.com, or call 1-800-323-9400.

ISBN 978-1-64158-204-9

Printed in China

26	25	24	23	22	21	20
7	6	5	4	3	2	1

contents

introduction

How Memorizing the Bible Empowers Us
for Discipleship and Mission

There is no standing still. Every gift, every increment of knowledge and insight I receive only drives me deeper into the word of God. . . . God has given us the Scripture, from which we are to discern God's will. The Scripture wants to be read and thought about, every day afresh.

DIETRICH BONHOEFFER

In 2018, Baeble Music released its list of the top karaoke songs of all time. You don't have to particularly like any of these songs or even have been born in the era when they were hits to have some of the lyrics of every one of these songs buried in your brain somewhere. From the list:[1]

1. "Mr. Brightside"—The Killers
2. "You Oughta Know"—Alanis Morissette
3. "I Will Always Love You"—Whitney Houston
4. "Don't Stop Believin'"—Journey
5. "Cheerleader"—OMI
6. "Wonderwall"—Oasis
7. "Ain't No Mountain High Enough"—Marvin Gaye and Tammi Terrell
8. "(You Make Me Feel Like) A Natural Woman"—Aretha Franklin
9. "Under Pressure"—Queen and David Bowie
10. "Lose Yourself"—Eminem

Go on, admit it. You heard a strain of "Just a small town girl / Livin' in a lonely world," didn't you? What about "And I wish to you joy and happiness / But above all this, I wish you love"? We might not know the whole song, and we might have even misheard or misremembered the lyrics, but a couple of lines like "Maybe, you're gonna be the one that saves me / And after all, you're my wonderwall"—well, they really stick, don't they? They're not called earworms for nothing.

What about lines from movies? We have friends who can quote whole scenes from *The Big Lebowski*. And everyone knows "I'll have what she's having," from *When Harry Met Sally . . .* , or "You complete me," from *Jerry Maguire*, or "I'm going to make him an offer he can't refuse," from *The Godfather*. It never ceases to amaze people what bits of useless dialogue they have rattling around in their brains. Jack Nicholson's courtroom testimony in *A Few Good Men* or Al Pacino's speech to the school board hearing in *Scent of a Woman*. Stupid gags from Ron Burgundy or Michael Scott. The esoteric musings of Dale Cooper. What's the use of knowing all that stuff? Is our memory just a repository for random bits of pointless data?

And yet memorization used to be a central part of learning. I (Michael) am just old enough to remember, when I was a young student in Australia, being made to recite long swathes of poetry or learn multiplication tables by rote. We were forced to memorize the periodic table of elements, and (for some reason) we had to be able to recount every river that flows into the eastern seaboard of Australia from north to south, and the major towns on its banks! I hated it—mostly because we got hit with a ruler if we got it wrong; things have changed a lot since then, thank goodness.

Memorization has a bad rap these days. Mainly because we know that information learned by rote in school is soon forgotten when we have no other use for it, but also because we live in an age when impromptu expression is more highly valued than memorized screeds.

Note how today people think public prayer is more meaningful if it's made up right there on the spot. We're suspicious of memorized liturgies because we assume they don't come from the heart. We prefer preachers who appear to be presenting extemporaneously to those who are either reading their notes or reciting them by rote. We don't trust politicians who are woodenly following a teleprompter. Our love of unrehearsed speech and our skepticism about memorized information have meant that no one commits anything to memory much anymore, except maybe PIN numbers.

And yet, in his treatise *On the Education of Children*, Plutarch claimed memory was a key component in the development of students:

> Above all, the memory of children should be trained and
> exercised; for this is, as it were, a storehouse of learning; and
> it is for this reason that the mythologists have made Memory
> the mother of the Muses, thereby intimating by an allegory
> that there is nothing in the world like memory for creating and
> fostering.[2]

In other words, the brain is a muscle, and if you want it to be strong enough to be creative and intelligent, you have to exercise it. According to Plutarch, rote learning is like burpees for the brain. We might forget useless information we memorized, but the process of learning it was good for us.

So how come I can't recite those Australian rivers in geographical order anymore, but if I walk into a pub and someone is singing Billy Joel's *Piano Man*, I know every word?

Poet and novelist Brad Leithauser has some thoughts on that. Writing for the *New Yorker* on the memorization of poetry, he says,

> The best argument for verse memorization may be that
> it provides us with knowledge of a qualitatively and
> physiologically different variety: you take the poem inside you,
> into your brain chemistry if not your blood, and you know it at
> a deeper, bodily level than if you simply read it off a screen.[3]

Whereas the recitation of poetry once achieved this, today it's pop music and dialogue from television and film that fill that role, conforming our hearts to the beat of their sometimes strange rhythm. So memory is important for the development of our brains, and poetry and pop songs are easier to memorize than Greek declensions or the periodic table (believe us!). But memorization is even more important than you might realize.

In her book *Heart Beats: Everyday Life and the Memorized Poem*, historian Catherine Robson explores how the memorization and recitation of poetry changed people from a previous era by changing the world in which they lived. It is a fascinating study of the history of rote learning and the public recitation of poetry, which was a mandatory teaching practice in England from around 1875 to the mid-1900s. She writes, "When we do not learn by heart, the heart does not feel the rhythms of poetry as echoes or variations of its own insistent beat."[4] Robson says there were a number of reasons for this focus on memorization:

- to foster a love of poetry and words;
- to boost a child's confidence through a mastery of elocution, while also purging the idioms and accents of lower-class speech;
- to exercise the brain, as Plutarch suggested; and
- to develop nationalistic zeal through the construction of a highly patriotic canon of poems that promote English values.

In other words, poetry recitation was used to make English kids properly English (as it was understood at the time). When Victorian-era children recited, "The boy stood on the burning deck . . ." they were doing more than exercising their brain. They were being *made* by the words.

Today we know that an insidious classist, nationalistic agenda inspired this British emphasis on memorization. Memorization in itself, then, isn't transformative. It's *what* you memorize that counts. A case could be (indeed *should* be) made that memorizing portions of the Bible can make Christian people properly Christian—not because the words are somehow magical, but because we're doing what Leithauser described: taking the words inside us, into our brains and our blood, so that "you know it at a deeper, bodily level than if you simply read it off a screen."

Expanding Our Kingdom Vision

More than fifty years ago, The Navigators released the Topical Memory System (TMS). It offered a simple system for memorizing Bible verses that help you live a new life, proclaim the gospel of Jesus Christ, rely on God's resources, be a disciple, and grow in Christlikeness. A sibling edition would focus on life issues: dealing with anger, sin, sex, money, suffering, and more. The verses chosen for memorization encouraged Christians to experience victory over sin, overcome fear and worry, enjoy boldness in witness, discover fresh depths of discipleship, and move from egotism to humility.

The TMS has a great story—decades of Christians whose faith lives have been enriched by its focus on divine love, transformed hearts, and foundational texts for an evangelical theology. But every tool has its limits, and we and others have observed that the verses included in the TMS don't touch on the more communal, social, and missional implications of the gospel. It is possible, then, for someone to do the good work of memorizing Scripture through a system like the TMS and come out on the other end assuming the gospel to be entirely individualistic, even egocentric.

This is not to say that the verses commended by the TMS are unimportant—they are the Word of God, after all—but there are many sections of Scripture also worthy of memorization that the TMS doesn't touch, and those sections can expand our Kingdom vision to include a life of justice and mercy, peacemaking and reconciliation.

Some people remain unconvinced that God calls us to a life of justice and reconciliation. Recently, I (Michael) tweeted something about God's call to the church to enact justice, and someone replied, "Where in Holy Scriptures does it state social justice? Christ said go and proclaim the gospel, not social justice. If Christ said proclaim social justice, I want Scripture to back it up" (actual tweet).

Fair enough. So I gave him some Scripture, to which he responded, "Okay. Just wanted clarity. So many people would not see that. Thank you" (also actual tweet).

As simple as that!

Rick Warren once said he immersed himself in the Bible and found two thousand verses on the poor. "How did I miss that? I went to Bible college, two seminaries, and I got a doctorate. How did I miss God's compassion for the poor? I was not seeing all the purposes of God."[5]

Memorizing Scripture shouldn't just help us internalize the key themes of our faith or overcome personal difficulties. We need an approach to Bible memorization that helps us embrace a Kingdom and missional theology, that leads us to whole-of-life discipleship, and that aids the Jesus-reflecting and activist Christian life. This book offers such an approach to Bible memory. It immerses you in many of the great (but often forgotten or neglected) themes of Scripture. These include hospitality, reconciliation, justice, peacemaking, compassion, love of enemies, sentness, and more. As you memorize (and visualize) and learn (relationally and through practices) key verses related to these biblical themes, you are empowered to live a surprising, "questionable" life.

In *Surprise the World*, I (Michael) wrote, "The fact is that we all recognize the need to live generous, hospitable, Spirit-led, Christlike lives as missionaries to our own neighborhoods. We want to live our faith out in the open for all to see."[6] That's where the five habits in *Surprise the World* come in (Bless, Eat, Listen, Learn, Sent—BELLS), as well as this fresh approach to Bible memorization. Together, these habits and this new commitment to Bible memorization "equip believers to see themselves as 'sent ones,' to foster a series of missional habits that shape our lives and values, and to propel us into the world confidently and filled with hope."[7]

This book offers an approach to Scripture memorization that helps us develop a radical Christian faith and an activist spirituality. Our approach to Bible memorization uses the latest science about how the brain works, how relationships form us, and how habits and practices shape us. Our method moves us away from an individualistic and intellectual form of Bible memory to one that aids us to be agents of reconciliation, prophets of justice, people of peace, and disciples who join with Jesus in his mission. As a companion to *Surprise the World*, this Bible memory approach is shaped around those five habits: blessing others, eating with others, listening to the Holy Spirit, learning Christ through focused study in the Gospels, and being sent. Starting in chapter 4, we'll introduce our system for memorizing Scripture, with particular passages we commend for broadening your biblical vision to profess and demonstrate the inbreaking Kingdom of God.

Many cultures commit their sacred, foundational texts to memory. For centuries in China, for example, boys were required to memorize the Dao. How important it is, then, for Christians who believe their texts to be the very words of God to do the same! Our hope is that instead of being easily able to draw to mind lyrics like "Oh I think that I found myself a cheerleader / She is always right there when I need her," you'll take verses like the following inside you, into your brain chemistry if not your blood, and know them at a deeper, bodily level:

> Your love, LORD, reaches to the heavens,
>   your faithfulness to the skies.
> Your righteousness is like the highest mountains,
>   your justice like the great deep.
>   You, LORD, preserve both people and animals.

PSALM 36:5-6

the beauty of memorized truth

When you read a hundred words a hundred times they get woven into your soul. . . . When we struggle with a text, it changes us. Why put things in memory? . . . We memorize to contemplate, not to show off.

ANDREW KERN

The German Baptist Brethren is a sect of Anabaptists who arrived in the United States in the 1720s. Back in the day, when Americans gave church movements funny nicknames like the Quakers and the Shakers, they were tagged the Dunkers.

Then in 1848 a bunch of Dunkers split from the original movement and called themselves the Church of God (now known as Church of the Brethren). To distinguish themselves from the original church they adopted the moniker the *New* Dunkers.

We're pretty sure young people growing up in the Church of the Brethren in recent times are loathe to refer to themselves as the New Dunkers—that is, until their national youth convention in 2014. On that occasion, pastor-activist Jarrod McKenna addressed the gathering of young people and christened them with a new name. They weren't just Dunkers, he said. They were Dunker Punks.

A punk is a young, radically countercultural person driven by nonconformity and committed to personal ideals rather than social norms. In short, a troublemaker. So, proclaimed McKenna, a Dunker Punk is a young member of the Church of the Brethren, but more specifically, of "a rebellious countercultural tradition that radically commits their life to living God's Calvary-shaped love in the power of the Spirit, to the glory of the Father."[1]

And what is the first order of business for a Dunker Punk, according to Jarrod McKenna? Mohawks? Safety pins through your nose? Inciting revolution? Spraying graffiti slogans around town? No, the first step in the Dunker Punk manual is to memorize the Sermon on the Mount. Yes, in that same address, having just renamed them, McKenna challenged them to learn three chapters of Scripture (Matthew 5–7) by heart.[2]

What?

Memorizing Scripture—letting it seep into your mind and soul—is standard procedure for those involved in justice-seeking, peacemaking, and reconciliation. Harriet Tubman did it. Sojourner Truth did it. Dorothy Day and Martin Luther King Jr. did it. In his journal from 1819, British parliamentarian and social reformer William Wilberforce made this entry: "Walked from Hyde Park Corner, repeating the 119th Psalm, in great comfort."[3]

Psalm 119 is 176 verses long! The Sermon on the Mount is 111 verses! Why are so many social reformers in the habit of memorizing such huge sections of the Bible? Allow us to share four reasons briefly.

1. To Honor Our Radical History

Bible memorization isn't just a Victorian-era religious practice akin to reciting "The Charge of the Light Brigade." Neither did it only come into vogue with the publication of the *Topical Memory System*. Dozens of Bible verses speak to the long history of God's people storing God's Word in their hearts and putting it into practice. Here are just a few examples:

Fix these words of mine in your hearts and minds; tie them as symbols on your hands and bind them on your foreheads.
DEUTERONOMY 11:18

Blessed is the one
    who does not walk in step with the wicked
or stand in the way that sinners take
    or sit in the company of mockers,
but whose delight is in the law of the LORD,
    and who meditates on his law day and night.
That person is like a tree planted by streams of water,
    which yields its fruit in season
and whose leaf does not wither—
    whatever they do prospers.
PSALM 1:1-3

I have hidden your word in my heart
    that I might not sin against you.
PSALM 119:11

Keep my commands and you will live;
    guard my teachings as the apple of your eye.
Bind them on your fingers;
    write them on the tablet of your heart.
PROVERBS 7:2-3

The ancient Hebrews emphasized the memorization of large sections of the *Torah* as a key feature in Jewish education. The focus was on oral teaching—which meant emphasizing repetition and memory as the cornerstones of education. This tradition was passed on to the early church and has stayed with us ever since.

The Gospels make it clear that Jesus memorized Scripture. The Gospels also show us that Jesus' astonishing, unconventional, weird, wise, and prophetic insights and actions were in response to his Father's will as revealed to him in prayer and in the Scriptures. The Sermon on the Mount (Matthew 5–7), Jesus' temptation in the wilderness (Matthew 4:1-11), and his mission statement (Luke 4:18-19) are just a few examples of this.

Of course, the Bible reminds us that meditating on and memorizing Scripture isn't enough. Storing God's Word in our hearts must lead to practices that deepen our discipleship, revitalize the church, and renew the world. James makes this clear in James 1:22-25, and there are many other passages that make a similar point. Bible memorization is an aid to discipleship and service and creativity. Throughout the history of the church, "those who practiced the crafts of memory used them—as all crafts are used—to *make* new things: prayers, meditations, sermons, pictures, hymns, stories, and poems."[4] Just like Plutarch said.

2. To Protect the Radical Heart

If we want to share our faith and be missional, then we must spend a lot of our time outside the church. That's the nature of our calling. We join networks and groups that are advocating social change. We interact with a lot of people who might share some of our values but reject our faith. In my (Michael's) previous book *Surprise the World*, I talk about how imperative it is for missional people to guard their hearts against sin and temptation.

> When I say "falling into sin," I don't necessarily mean getting drunk or running off with your neighbor's spouse (although of course we're never immune to making such choices). I'm referring to the much less dramatic but far more prevalent sins of fear and laziness . . . [which] are mission killers.[5]

Fear of persecution, fear of causing offense, fear of looking stupid . . . all these fears and more will kill your commitment to the cause of

Christ. Likewise, the kind of laziness that sees you retract into your safe world, losing interest in the struggle for social change, telling yourself you need to be taken care of first, will shut down your radical zeal. The perfect antidote is to immerse yourself in the words of Scripture, drawing on them in times of temptation, meditating on them when you feel weak. The psalmist writes, "How can a young person stay on the path of purity? By living according to your word" (Psalm 119:9).

German theologian Dietrich Bonhoeffer knew this only too well. "It is never sufficient," he wrote, "simply to have read God's Word. It must penetrate deep within us, dwell in us, like the Holy of Holies in the Sanctuary, so that we do not sin in thought, word, or deed."[6]

Jesus resisted the tempter's wiles by quoting memorized Scripture, all of it from the book of Deuteronomy. This story serves an important function in the Gospel. By resisting temptation and quoting the words of Moses, Jesus is revealed to be the new, improved liberator. Jesus does what Moses knew but could not do. He out-Moseses Moses. The words of Deuteronomy provide him with a reminder of his task. They are his North Star, focusing him afresh on his purpose and destiny, to be the liberator of humankind. Little wonder that he memorized it. He shows himself to have a head full of Scripture.

Learning and reciting the Bible is not some kind of magic spell that wards off bad thoughts. But the words of Scripture can do for us what they did for Jesus in the wilderness: articulate our identity and purpose. Learn the Bible, and bring to mind these shaping lines—the words given to us by God—that have brought us to life and propelled us into mission.

As we said in the introduction, the British school system promoted poetry memorization as a vehicle for shaping patriotic souls who spoke "the king's English," as it was termed. In a much more positive way, memorizing Scripture shapes our values and vision as followers of Christ and strengthens us in times of weakness and temptation.

3. To Shape the Radical Vision

The mission of God's people is to alert everyone everywhere to the universal reign of Christ, which includes both announcement and demonstration. We'll address this more in the next chapter. But while many younger Christians have embraced an understanding of Christian mission that includes both evangelism and social justice, they can be a little vague on the biblical basis for believing that.

John M. Perkins—community organizer, civil rights activist, and cofounder of the Christian Community Development Association (CCDA)—is a third-grade dropout. His mother died when he was a baby, and his father abandoned him to be raised by his grandmother and extended family, all of whom worked as sharecroppers in Mississippi. And yet Perkins has become one of the leading Christian voices in addressing issues like poverty, injustice, racism, and materialism. Through his example—as well as through his preaching, his writing, and his leadership institute—he has influenced countless people to become committed to the renewal and restoration of their communities. His secret? He memorizes the Bible. If you've heard John Perkins preach (or if, like us, you've had the opportunity to have a personal conversation with him), you'll know his speech is dripping with references from the Bible. In an interview with *Christianity Today*, Perkins spoke about how it began.

> I began to read it. And what I was reading I began to
> understand. And it stuck there. You never heard me teach, but
> as I teach the Scriptures I can memorize the relevant Scriptures.
> I can just take a whole text and memorize it, not so much as
> you would think of memorize. I memorize it as I read it, if my
> brain comprehended it. . . . Those passages are still in my head
> and in my memory, in blocks. . . . So I have the Bible sort of in
> textual order in my head, and that makes it easy then to pull up
> and explain. That is no doubt a gift, but the brain also has great

capacity to absorb. Then of course I think once you give your life to God I think the Spirit is there, wooing you on.[7]

Scripture memorization helps to create a font of knowledge from which to draw during the difficult days in the field. My (Graham's) great-grandfather John McKittrick was born in Glasgow in 1903 and immigrated to Australia when he was twenty-one, coming to faith in Jesus Christ during the sea voyage to Sydney. He arrived in his new homeland resolved to serve God with all his strength. In 1933, he began working with Sydney City Mission, serving among Sydney's homeless and most vulnerable. The rest of his life would be spent among the destitute, alcoholics, sex workers, and ex-offenders. Passionate about evangelism and social justice, he personally led many thousands of people to Christ. I remember spending time in his home when I was a boy, which was often filled with the kind of people Jesus spent his life with: the addicted, the forgotten, the shunned, the feared, the exploited, the violent, the outcast. It was a warm, welcoming, and healing home for all people, no matter what life had thrown at them. Bible reading and memorization fueled John's passion for justice and for welcoming and serving the broken.

I vividly remember catching my great-grandfather early in the mornings on his knees before his Bible, praying and memorizing Scripture. He would say, "Every single day I go into God's Word and meet Jesus. Every day Jesus speaks to me and fills me with his love. His Word calls me to act justly and love mercy and walk humbly with my God. Jesus will never let you go! Follow him, share his love, and let Jesus and his Word transform your life!" I was only eight or nine at the time, but the witness of John McKittrick's Scripture-soaked and missional life has stayed with me ever since.

Bible reading and memorization energizes and galvanizes a life committed to proclaiming the gospel, caring for the poor, welcoming the outcast, reconciling enemies, and seeking a more just, equitable, and whole society. Memorizing Scripture empowers and aids missional churches and disciples.

4. To Comfort the Radical Mind

Henry Martyn was a nineteenth-century missionary to India and Persia. A Cambridge graduate, he translated the whole of the New Testament into Urdu, Persian, and Judeo-Persian. He also translated the Psalms into Persian and the Book of Common Prayer into Urdu. But he was also a troubled soul. And the hardships of missionary life only made things worse. In his letters he regularly refers to being "full of anxiety" and "most dispirited" by "these melancholy effects upon my mind."[8]

One of his recurring concerns was for the "unprofitableness" of his life. This is a common source of unease among missionaries and those serving Christ in the world. Because the results of our labors are so difficult to see or assess, we regularly ask ourselves, Is my work making any difference? Is it at all profitable? What's the point of continuing this struggle?

Martyn's primary source of comfort came from prayer and from reciting memorized Scripture. On January 8, 1804, he wrote, "The Psalms this evening were in entire unison with my feelings. I could have repeated those words many more times, 'Why art thou so heavy, O my soul, why art thou so disquieted within me?'"[9] Earlier, on December 28, 1803, he recorded, "Found some devotion in learning a part of Psalm 119."[10]

Memorized Scriptures can be like powerful time-release capsules. In the midst of depression or despondency they can be drawn to mind to ease a difficult situation. Many Christian leaders have testified to the life-changing power of memorizing the Bible. Dallas Willard, for example, says, "Bible memorization is absolutely fundamental to spiritual formation. If I had to choose between all the disciplines of the spiritual life, I would choose Bible memorization, because it is a fundamental way of filling our minds with what it needs."[11]

In his memoir about the seven years he spent as a prisoner of war in North Vietnam, pilot Howard Rutledge described the dreadful conditions he and other American servicemen endured at the hands of the

Vietcong. As well as the unsanitary and uncomfortable surroundings, the meager diet, and the torture, Rutledge describes the battle to keep his mind alert, to not give in to despair. He desperately tried to recall passages of Scripture but couldn't.

It took prison to show me how empty life is without God, and so I had to go back in my memory to those Sunday-school days . . . in Tulsa, Oklahoma. If I couldn't have a Bible and hymnbook, I would try to rebuild them in my mind. . . . I tried desperately to recall snatches of Scripture, sermons, the gospel choruses from childhood, and the hymns we sang in church. . . . How I struggled to recall those Scriptures and hymns! I had spent my first eighteen years in . . . Sunday school, and I was amazed at how much I could recall; regrettably, I had not seen then the importance of memorizing verses from the Bible. . . . Now, when I needed them, it was too late. I never dreamed that I would spend almost seven years (five of them in solitary confinement) in a prison in North Vietnam or that thinking about one memorized verse could have made the whole day bearable. One portion of a verse I did remember was, "Thy word have I hid in my heart." How often I wished I had really worked to hide God's Word in my heart.[12]

We share Rutledge's experience not to prepare you for a time when you'll be deprived of a Bible but as a warning from one who wished his heart was more full of Scripture in times of extreme loneliness, depression, or stress. Brad Leithauser writes of memorization (in his case, poetry) as "a sort of larder, laid up against the hungers of an extended period of solitude":

My late colleague Joseph Brodsky . . . [had] been grateful for every scrap of poetry he had in his head during his enforced exile in the Arctic, banished there by a Soviet government that did not know what to do with his genius and that, in a symbolic embrace of a national policy of brain drain, expelled him from the country in 1972.[13]

Memorization and More

Before we give you the incorrect impression that Bible memorization is some silver bullet for discipleship and mission, allow us to sound some gentle warnings. There should be much more to your use of the Bible than being able to recite certain verses by heart.

In his book *Scripture and the Authority of God*, New Testament scholar N.T. Wright explores the role the Bible plays in the life of the church and makes a series of recommendations for how it should be read. We reiterate them here because we agree that Scripture memorization should be done alongside the following five ways of reading the Bible.

1. Read the Bible in Context

"When I first became a devout follower of Jesus," Wright recalls, "my Christian friends strongly encouraged me to memorize certain passages of Scripture."[14] He took to it with enthusiasm. But he notes that the verses he was encouraged to learn—verses such as "There is therefore no condemnation for those who are in Christ Jesus" (Romans 8:1, esv); "Therefore, since we have been justified through faith, we have peace with God through our Lord Jesus Christ" (Romans 5:1); and "Therefore do not let sin reign in your mortal body" (Romans 6:12)—tended to present a narrow, individualistic faith focused on personal redemption.

> These are fabulous verses. . . . Each text had a "therefore" in it. It never occurred to me at the time that the "therefore" was there for a reason. I was encouraged in what I knew and didn't know what I didn't know. All was well until I started reading the text in context.[15]

As he puts it, he needed to start memorizing the "therefores" as well. Every memorized verse or passage must be understood in its larger context (its chapter; its book; and its historical, cultural, and canonical setting). But Wright goes even further, saying that our own contexts as readers affect our understanding of Scripture, leading us to focus on some sections of the Bible while ignoring others. This has been proven throughout history. Wright says,

> Such a contextual reading is in fact an incarnational reading of Scripture, paying attention to the full humanity both of the text and its readers. This must be undertaken in the prayer that the "divinity"—the "inspiration" of Scripture, and the Spirit's power at work within the Bible-reading church—will thereby be discovered afresh.[16]

2. Read the Bible in Church

Wright, a former Anglican bishop, says that because "the primary place where the church hears Scripture is during corporate worship . . . we must work at making sure we read Scripture properly in public, with appropriate systems for choosing what to read and appropriate training to make sure those who read do so to best effect."[17] Readers from a less liturgical tradition might take issue with that statement, but even Baptists and Pentecostals could acknowledge the value of the whole community gathering together to hear the Word of God read publicly.

3. Read the Bible Studiously

We all need to commit ourselves to the personal *study* of Scripture, not only the memorization of certain sections. In a powerful statement, Dr. Wright says, "For all of this to make the deep, life-changing, Kingdom-advancing sense it is supposed to, it is vital that ordinary Christians read, encounter, and study Scripture for themselves, in groups and individually."[18]

4. Read the Bible with Scholars

There's a difference between reading the Bible for pleasure and for insight, not unlike reading a novel or a newspaper, and studying Scripture in light of the latest scholarship. Wright insists we honor the original meaning of the Bible; in some cases doing so requires the insights of professional scholars. Not everything in the Bible is to be taken literally. Some of it is in the form of poetry, songs, acrostics, and apocalyptic imagery. He says, "Biblical scholarship is a great gift of God to the church, aiding it in its task of going ever deeper into the meaning of scripture and so being refreshed and energized for the tasks to which we are called in and for the world."[19]

5. Read the Bible with Pastors

As a member of a local congregation, one that reads the Bible together on Sundays and throughout the week in small groups, you are learning under the pastoral direction of those set aside for that task. Your church's leaders are, it is hoped, qualified and experienced to shepherd you and the others in your community to keep the teachings of the Bible at the heart of the church's life.

With these recommendations in place, you can see the added value of memorization. Combining rote learning with Christian worship on Sundays, midweek Bible studies, and private research fulfills N. T. Wright's emphasis on both individual and corporate readings of Scripture and hopefully integrates Scripture into your daily life as you seek to be a disciple who is generous, hospitable, Spirit-led, Christlike, and missionary.

a big, beautiful, expansive gospel

*The gospel is the work of God to restore humans to union
with God and communion with others, in the context
of a community for the good of others and the world.*

SCOT MCKNIGHT

In 1807, the British publishing house Law and Gilbert began producing a special edition of the Bible for a missionary organization named the Society for the Conversion of Negro Slaves. It was claimed to be for evangelistic use among enslaved Africans in the British West Indies, now the Caribbean. But more than simply educating slaves in the Christian faith, this Bible had a second, more insidious purpose: It was intended to preserve the system of slavery.

The title was a giveaway: *Parts of the Holy Bible, selected for the use of the Negro Slaves, in the British West-India Islands.* Not the whole Bible, just parts. "About 90 percent of the Old Testament is missing [and] 50 percent of the New Testament is missing. . . . Put in another way, there are 1,189 chapters in a standard protestant Bible. This Bible contains only 232."[1]

It is worth noting which sections of the Bible were redacted. Anything that would appear to suggest slavery was a bad thing was removed. So the stories of Moses telling Pharaoh to "Let my people go" were expunged. But references to Joseph's enslavement in Egypt were included—presumably because they depict things working out well for the adult Joseph. You can't find Paul's words from Galatians 3:28, "There is neither Jew nor Gentile, neither slave nor free, nor is there male and female, for you are all one in Christ Jesus," in this edition because all passages that emphasized unity and equality among believers were excised. No book of Revelation either. You can't have slaves reading about a new heaven and a new earth in which justice will be established and evil will be punished. Put simply, the colonizers and slave owners were giving African slaves a "holy" book that taught them to be satisfied with their station in life and look forward to heaven when they died.

The timing of the publication of this abridged version of the Bible is significant: Just three years beforehand, a slave revolt in Haiti had driven European settlers and slave owners from the island (the most successful slave revolt in recent history). It created enormous disquiet across the Caribbean, including places like Jamaica, Barbados, and Antigua. Americans and Europeans were terrified at the thought of similar uprisings elsewhere. Distributing a Bible that quelled slave uprisings was an elegant, if evil, solution.

There are only three extant copies of the Slave Bible still in existence. One copy belongs to Fisk University in Nashville; the other two are located in the United Kingdom. In 2018, when the Museum of the Bible in Washington, DC, established an exhibit featuring the borrowed Fisk copy, it created quite a stir. People were outraged that the Holy Scriptures had been tampered with in this way and for this purpose. But it is worth acknowledging that in a far less obvious way, many of us also only read the sections of the Bible we prefer.

Where You Stand Will Determine What You See

Without actually excising sections of the Bible, it is possible to have portions invisible to your gaze. A newspaper reporter was sent to Birmingham, Alabama, to report on the deaths of four little girls in the 16th Street Baptist Church bombing on Sunday, September 15, 1963. The reporter took an unusual angle on the story, calling every minister in the city and asking them what passage of Scripture they used as the text for their sermon on the day of the bombing. Every white pastor in Birmingham was preaching from the Epistles; every black preacher was teaching on Isaiah or the Minor Prophets or Revelation. In other words, whites were studying the more abstract theology of Paul, while the black churches dwelt in the more communal, justice-focused, future-oriented sections of the Bible.

Robert McAfee Brown was noted for saying, "Remember that: 1) where you stand will determine what you will see; 2) whom you stand with will determine what you hear; and 3) what you see and hear will determine what you say and how you act."[2] He was referring to the white, middle-class church's limited understanding of poverty and racism. But Brown's maxim is true in all manner of circumstances. We can all be narrow-minded in our perspectives, and we can all be inadvertently limited in our reading of Scripture.

If our favorite verses include discussions of sin, forgiveness, redemption, and heaven but don't address justice, peacemaking, and the renewal of all things, we might have embraced a beautiful set of doctrines while overlooking other people.

It is interesting to consider the outcomes of the annual review of the most popular verses on online Bible apps like YouVersion or Bible Gateway. Considering that Bible Gateway has racked up 920 million searches on its site, and YouVersion has tracked more than 1.7 billion highlights, bookmarks, and notes on more than 350 million devices across the world, it provides a helpful insight into what verses people are reading.[3] Here are the top verses on YouVersion in recent years:

- 2015—Proverbs 3:5-6: "Trust in the LORD with all your heart and lean not on your own understanding; in all your ways submit to him, and he will make your paths straight."
- 2016—Romans 8:28: "And we know that in all things God works for the good of those who love him, who have been called according to his purpose."

- 2017—Joshua 1:9: "Have I not commanded you? Be strong and courageous. Do not be afraid; do not be discouraged, for the Lord your God will be with you wherever you go."

In 2018, the most-read verse on the Bible Gateway website was Jeremiah 29:11: "'For I know the plans I have for you,' declares the Lord, 'plans to prosper you and not to harm you, plans to give you hope and a future.'" On YouVersion it was Isaiah 41:10: "So do not fear, for I am with you; do not be dismayed, for I am your God. I will strengthen you and help you; I will uphold you with my righteous right hand."

Can you detect a theme? God being with you wherever you go; God holding you in his hand; being strengthened; things working out for the good; your paths being made straight; prospering. Combine this with the most popular word searches on Bible Gateway (love, peace, faith, Holy Spirit, forgive, truth) and you see the pattern appears to be a preference for uplifting and reassuring verses.

YouVersion founder Bobby Gruenewald reflected on these results: "People worldwide are continuing to turn to the Bible in search of comfort, encouragement, and hope."[4] We agree. And we think it's great. It's important that Christians should take comfort in the encouraging words they find in Scripture. But we're concerned that people might be missing the encouragement of verses that express God's heart for justice, racial reconciliation, welcoming the stranger, feeding the hungry, and the end of tyranny and oppression. We are not only redeemed people; we are redeemed to be agents of reconciliation, prophets of justice, and people of peace. All Christians need to immerse themselves in a whole-of-life discipleship that both celebrates personal forgiveness and anticipates the coming Kingdom. In this regard, we believe it's important to resist the following temptations:

- to read the Bible individualistically rather than communally;
- to read only sections that reinforce our existing biases rather than being confronted and changing;

- to narrow our understanding of the gospel rather than pursuing a holistic gospel;
- to treat the Bible as a doctrinal textbook rather than seeking a whole-of-life application of its content;
- to divorce Scripture from context rather than reading and applying it in context;
- to focus on verses that promise personal gratification and eternal security rather than wrestling with texts that stand up to the challenges of a world without Christ.

We hope the memorization of the Scriptures included in this book will help to broaden your view of the gospel and see God's extraordinary story of love and redemption in its biggest possible conception. So, as you begin a process of Bible immersion, we want to sound a few words of warning about not shrinking the gospel.

1. Don't Accept a Reductionist Gospel

For too many Christians, the gospel is just information for how to go to heaven when you die. While the gospel includes a concern about the eternal destiny of all peoples, we think it is reductionist to limit the gospel to only this concern. Tim Keller writes, "The gospel is the good news that God himself has come to rescue and renew *all of creation* through the work of Jesus Christ on our behalf."[5]

God's plan of redemption is not only for lost souls, but for the whole of creation. Indeed, it is a mistake to think of Jesus' life, death, and resurrection as God's plan B for the world, as though human sin caught God unawares and he had to resort to drastic measures. Lesslie Newbigin says, "[The Bible] is concerned with the completion of God's purpose in the creation of the world. It is not—to put it crudely—concerned with offering a way of escape for the redeemed soul out of history, but with the action of God to bring history to its true end."[6]

God is sovereign. Everything is under his control. He is directing history and participating with the redeemed community to bring every-thing to the true end that he always intended. So it is reductionist to insist that God is concerned only with saving souls. We limit the gospel when we drive a wedge between personal salvation and social transformation, between evangelism and social justice. N. T. Wright explains it this way:

> The mission of the church is nothing more or less than the outworking, in the power of the Spirit, of Jesus's bodily resurrection and thus the anticipation of the time when God will fill the earth with his glory, transform the old heavens and earth into the new, and raise his children from the dead to populate and rule over the redeemed world he has made.
>
> If that is so, mission must urgently recover from its long-term schizophrenia. . . . The split between saving souls and doing good in the world is a product not of the Bible or the gospel but of the cultural captivity of both.[7]

2. Don't Fall for an Individualistic Gospel

It's very tempting to see yourself at the center of God's plans. Discouraged or downtrodden people will search online Bible platforms for verses about God's love for them without recognizing that the texts were writ-ten to readers in the plural. Take Bible Gateway's second most popu-lar verse of 2019 for example: "'For I know the plans I have for you,' declares the LORD, 'plans to prosper you and not to harm you, plans to give you hope and a future'" (Jeremiah 29:11). This message from God wasn't written to you personally. It was written to the people of Israel to sustain them through seventy years of exile in Babylon. The "you" in that verse is better translated "*y'all*." Taking a verse that refers to God's faithfulness to Israel and applying it solely to your confusion about the next steps in your life is to overindividualize or personalize your reading of the Bible.

The gospel isn't chiefly about you. The gospel is news about the sovereign rule of the triune God. This news must be accepted by us in faithful, grateful obedience so that it can shape us into a redeemed society of persons who trust in God's present rule, hope for its final revelation, and are used by God to fashion foretastes of that rule right now.

This isn't to say God isn't concerned with individuals. Jesus told parables about the Kingdom of God being like a shepherd rescuing *one* lost sheep, or a woman finding *one* lost coin, or a father welcoming home *one* lost son (Luke 15). The gospel is news about the character of God and his reign and rule. But it is also about how individuals are found by God and restored to a redeemed community.

Missiologist David Bosch captures this in his definition of evangelism, which he says is concerned with both individuals and communities, and which always results in redeemed persons reorienting their lives not only on God but also on others:

> Evangelism is that dimension and activity of the church's mission which, by word and deed and in the light of particular conditions and a particular context, offers every person and community, everywhere, a valid opportunity to be directly challenged to a radical reorientation of their lives, a reorientation which involves such things as deliverance from slavery to the world and its powers; embracing Christ as Savior and Lord; becoming a living member of his community, the church; being enlisted into his service of reconciliation, peace, and justice on earth; and being committed to God's purpose of placing all things under the rule of Christ.[8]

3. Don't Preach a Punitive Gospel

Most evangelistic presentations emphasize the punitive element of the gospel. They emphasize the fact that God created us to be perfect, but that we (all humankind) have sinned and come under the condemnation of God. The Good News: Our sin and its consequences are transferred (imputed) to Jesus on the cross—there will be no condemnation for those in Christ. If we trust in the atoning death of Jesus, we will live a holy life by the power of the Spirit, waiting, hoping, and persevering until the end.

In this formulation, the gospel is focused on how to avoid hell when you die. The gospel comes to sound like it's principally a way to avoid condemnation and eternal punishment. One well-known evangelistic technique involves asking people, "If you were to die today, where would you spend eternity?" The focus is on dodging God's wrath.

In his book *The Suburban Captivity of the Church*, Tim Foster contrasts the more conventional, punitive gospel with what he refers to as a "telic gospel," which focuses on how God recovers his purposes for the world in spite of human fallenness. The term "telic" comes from the Greek *telos*, which means an end or purpose. From it we derive the term *teleology*, the study of objects in light of their purpose. By referring to the gospel as telic, Foster is saying we should view the biblical narrative in light of God's purpose of setting everything to rights. He explains it this way:

> The gospel is the announcement that God's purposes are being fulfilled; that the old world order is finished and his new order (which is called "the kingdom of God" in the Bible) is arriving through the life death and resurrection of Jesus.[9]

A simple way to compare the typical punitive gospel and Foster's telic approach is with this table:[10]

	Punitive Gospel	Telic Gospel
The beginning	God created us to be perfect.	God created the world according to his good purposes.
The problem	Human sin brings us under wrath.	Human sin opens the door for evil, undermining God's purposes.

	Punitive Gospel	Telic Gospel
The solution	Our sin and its consequences are transferred (imputed) to Jesus on the cross.	Jesus took our punishment. He conquers evil, brings forgiveness, and defeats death.
The future	There will be no condemnation for those in Christ.	There will be a new social and political order according to God's purposes.
The present	We trust in the atoning death of Jesus. We live a holy life by the power of the Spirit. We wait, hope, and persevere.	The new order has begun with the resurrection of Jesus. We live in the light of the future in the power of the Spirit.

If you look at the bottom box in the table, you'll see that a strong focus on avoiding punishment means that our current existence is marked by hopeful waiting and perseverance. We are free from condemnation; our ultimate reward is in heaven. But a more telic gospel invites redeemed sinners to join God in living out his purposes—the purposes for which we were created—now!

A good illustration of the difference between sharing a punitive gospel and a telic gospel can be summed up by this social media post by Daniel Hill, the senior pastor at River City Community Church in Chicago:

Funny interaction at breakfast today. An old-timer evangelized me and asked if I was confident that Jesus lives in my heart, and confident that I'm going to heaven when I die. I thanked him and said I was indeed confident.

Then I asked if I could pose a similar but different question to him. In addition to having Jesus in his heart, was he confident that he was connected meaningfully to the heart of Jesus? And in addition to the confidence of being in heaven when he died, was he confident he was pursuing heaven on earth right now in meaningful ways?

He told me that was not the gospel message, so we had a nice, friendly debate about the Lord's Prayer ("Thy kingdom come. Thy will be done on earth as it is in heaven."), about deep faith (Christ being "in us" but also the huge NT emphasis on us being "in Christ"), and how to hold a view of the gospel that integrates eternal life with life here and now.[11]

The "old-timer" was presenting a punitive gospel—information about how to go to heaven. What was important to him was whether you had Jesus in your heart and if you were ready to die. Dan's response is more telic: It's concerned with "connecting meaningfully to the heart of Jesus," and "pursuing heaven on earth right now," and "integrating eternal life with life here and now."

As Tim Foster says, "The call of the gospel is to believe that this new order has arrived in Jesus, and in believing to live according to this new way in the power of the spirit."[12] Or as we once heard Derwin Gray say in a sermon, "It's God's story, and he invites us into it. And when we lose ourselves in his story, that's when we find our purpose."

4. Don't Believe in an Anthropocentric Gospel

Because the gospel is good news about the reign of God through Christ, it is unreservedly theocentric (God-centered), not anthropocentric (human-centered). This isn't to say there aren't implications for human beings, as we've pointed out, but those implications emerge from belief in the kingship of Jesus and the inexorable unfurling of his Kingdom. As you're memorizing Bible verses, we want you to remember how they point to the following realities of the Kingdom of God.

The reign of God is above and beyond history. God initiated it, God owns it, God directs it. The reign of God is beyond the control and purview of the church. God's rule is total, utter, and complete. Part of what it means to be committed to God's purpose of placing all things under the rule of Christ is to see that we are called to acknowledge the ultimate sovereignty of God. The Kingdom, then, is God's gift to be gratefully accepted. It is the ground upon which our Christian faith and life is built. Our response should be gratitude, worship, and devotion.

The reign of God has entered into history and is unfolding within time and space. Thankfully, the Kingdom is near. It is unfolding among us. This was the essence of Jesus' mission and the content of the message he gave the disciples when he sent them out to every town: "Tell them, 'The kingdom of God has come near to you'" (Luke 10:9). While God's reign is total, utter, and complete above and beyond history, within time and space we see it only fitfully, partially, and mysteriously. Nonetheless, we take it by faith as a present fact, and we participate in it as we give our allegiance to God and seek to do his will on earth. It is our task; we pray for it, and we work for it.

The reign of God is seen fully at the end, or beyond the end, of history. We wait in hope for its complete coming, whether this occurs by gradual change or by an abrupt termination of earthly history. But we don't wait passively. As we pointed out previously, we have been enlisted into God's service of reconciliation, peace, and justice on earth.

For as Often as You Eat the Bread and Drink the Cup

Jesus gave us a perfect way to recall all this when he instituted the Lord's Supper (or Communion or whatever your tradition calls it). The early Christians called it the Love Feast, and it was a practice of communal memorization. Every time they met, the early church would share a meal together, not unlike a potluck supper today. Everyone was welcome at their table. The poor, including slaves who couldn't afford to contribute anything, ate as much as the rich. In the middle of the feast, a leader would take bread and raise her or his cup and repeat certain memorized words, elevating the simple meal to a sacred moment. The words they would use were penned by Paul, but he of course had borrowed them from Christ (Mark 14:22-25; Luke 22:18-20):

> For I received from the Lord what I also passed on to you:
> The Lord Jesus, on the night he was betrayed, took bread, and
> when he had given thanks, he broke it and said, "This is my
> body, which is for you; do this in remembrance of me." In the
> same way, after supper he took the cup, saying, "This cup is
> the new covenant in my blood; do this, whenever you drink it,
> in remembrance of me." For whenever you eat this bread and
> drink this cup, you proclaim the Lord's death until he comes.
> 1 CORINTHIANS 11:23-26

The Lord's Supper is a memorized celebration of God's reign. And it includes all three elements we outlined above:

- It recognizes that God's reign is above and beyond history.
- It celebrates that the Kingdom of God has broken into time and space, most perfectly in the Incarnation, the teaching, and the death and resurrection of Jesus.
- It invites us to participation in the Kingdom until the end of history.

Every time the early Christians ate and drank together, they were refreshing their collective memory about the big, beautiful, expansive gospel of Jesus.

It's Time We Proclaimed a Big, Beautiful, Expansive Gospel

For many people, the gospel they've heard hasn't been good news. A gospel that focuses only on personal sin and individual eternal destinies doesn't sound like good news to those who are enslaved, poor, and marginalized. How can a reductionist, punitive, individualistic, and human-centered gospel ever be good news to those suffering from modern-day human trafficking and slavery? How can it be good news to those surviving domestic violence or those suffering the devastating effects of climate change? How can it be good news for indigenous and native peoples who've had their lands stolen, or to African Americans who survived slavery and social injustices? Only a big, beautiful, expansive gospel can be good news to all people.

Lisa Sharon Harper says, "If one's gospel falls mute when facing people who need good news the most—the impoverished, the oppressed, and the broken—then it's no gospel at all."[13] This is why Lisa says we need to recover "the very good gospel"—the gospel we find in the Gospels, which included "systemic justice, peace between people groups, and freedom for the oppressed. The good news was both about the *coming* of the Kingdom of God and the *character* of that Kingdom. It was about what God's Kingdom looked like. It was about what citizenship in God's Kingdom requires. The biblical gospel writers' good news was about the restoration of shalom."[14]

This "very good gospel" emphasizes *shalom* (God's peace, justice, freedom, wholeness, and restoration) between us and God and between people. This gospel proclaims shalom between genders, between humans and creation, between races and nations, and for broken churches, neighborhoods, and families. Such *gospel shalom* is truly a big, beautiful, expansive gospel—good news!

Memorized words and practices can help us live into that expansive gospel. They can help us bring peace, justice, healing, and reconciliation to our homes, churches, public squares, neighborhoods, and societies. They can inspire us to be ambassadors of the very good news! But memorized Bible verses will do that only if we're drinking from the whole well of Scripture and not just the sections we like.

the art of memory

Memory is like a spiderweb that catches new information. The more it catches, the bigger it grows. And the bigger it grows, the more it catches.

JOSHUA FOER

Like Columbus Day in the United States, the date on which Australia was first settled by British colonists is a contested holiday. Australia Day is celebrated by many Australians as the founding of the nation, but for indigenous Australians it is regarded as the beginning of the British invasion of their territory. Amid the many protest marches and opprobrium that the day attracts, a group of Aboriginal Christians have launched an annual prayer service—a time of acknowledgment, lament, and mourning—during which they challenge the Australian church to hear and respond to Aboriginal people's call for voice, treaty, and truth.

One of the highlights of the 2019 service was when our friends Helen Wright and Bianca Manning sang their own composition, "Sister, Why Do You Weep?" Helen is white and Bianca is a Gomeroi Aboriginal woman. The structure of the song suggests that a white Australian is asking an indigenous sister why she is grieving:

Sister, why do you weep?
I weep for my people
Sister, why do you weep?
I weep for my land
Sister, why do you weep?
I weep for my song
A cry goes out across the land,
We're broken.

It moved many of us to tears. For days after the service, I (Graham) was walking around the house and neighborhood singing "Sister, Why Do You Weep?" word for word. I would often stop and cry as I remembered the power of that night and of Bianca's and Helen's voices. How did I memorize those words so quickly? How did they go so deep? The words of the song and the power of the night combined to lodge the lyrics deep in my heart and mind. We call this the art of memory.

The art of memory is often practiced in the memory of art. There's a natural correspondence between what we perceive as art and what we remember that more purely rational or intellectual material doesn't as easily achieve. We remember art because art is memorable, and art is memorable because the experience of it creates a memory for us.

Art and Holy Scriptures have a lot of parallels, then, in that they are not artificially constrained by preconceived standards and conventions, they engage both the intellect and the emotions (and the spirit), and they are often (maybe mostly) invested in real, earthy things and yet aspire to the transcendent. So while there is a science to how the memory works, and particularly how Bible memory works, we are well served by thinking of memorization more fully as an art.

To nurture the art of memory, we need to do six things.

1. *Learn* from the latest science about how the brain works and learns and how we form memories.

2. *Love* people deeply, within the context of a Christian community that forms your heart, life, and memory.

3. *Linger* with the Bible texts through carefully designed habits that shape you and encourage the Bible to go deeply into your heart.

4. *Link* stories, novels, art, poetry, nature, beauty, and current events with these Bible verses by making creative and imaginative links.

5. *Live* the verses out in your personal discipleship and in your family, ministry, and neighborhood by seeking to live a life committed to justice, peace, love, and world-changing discipleship.

6. *Lean* on the Holy Spirit for his enabling us to memorize the verses and live them out.

Let's look at each of these six features of *the art of Bible memory.*

1. Learn: Seek Fresh Approaches as You Memorize

We remember what we learn creatively.

In the 1950s and 1960s, educationalist Benjamin Bloom developed a series of learning objectives that have underpinned the education system ever since. They are called Bloom's Taxonomy. Bloom and his team identified six essential levels of learning—levels that successful students needed to reach: remember, understand, apply, analyze, evaluate, and create.[1] Each level is foundational to and integrated with the others. We move from memory to understanding, to applying, to analyzing, to evaluating, and then to creating. Memorization wasn't minimized in this model; Bloom said it serves as the basis for high levels of thinking and learning and creating.

In her book *The Secrets to Top Students*, Stefanie Weisman looked at the latest research and science to see what makes for a top student. She spoke with Rhodes scholars, Goldwater scholars, Fulbright award winners, college valedictorians, Intel Science Fair finalists, and National Spelling Bee champions. What she discovered was that they all trained themselves to memorize. They valued memorization because it enhanced their reasoning and improved their performance. Weisman writes,

> Memorization has gotten a bad rap recently. Lots of students, and even some educators, say that being able to reason is more important than knowing facts; and besides, why bother committing things to memory when you've got Google? My response to this—after I've finished inwardly groaning—is that of course reasoning is important, but that doesn't mean you shouldn't know facts as well. It's not like you have to choose between one or the other. Besides, facts give you a foundation on which to reason about things.[2]

Serious students of Scripture should be like serious math students or science students. Memorization should play no less a part of our learning journey. So, seek fresh approaches as you memorize the Bible. Learn from the latest science about how the brain works, how our brains learn, how we form memories. Adapt and refine your approach to memorizing the Bible as new insights emerge. This is about *learning* to memorize. Don't get stuck in one way of memorizing. Mix it up. Try new things. Listen to what works for others. What works for others may help you, but you need to discover what works best for you. Adapt. Change. Be flexible. Be a lifelong learner. *We remember what we learn creatively.*

2. Love: Grow through Relationships as You Memorize

We remember what we learn together.

In modern Western cultures, we have too often made learning and memorizing an individual affair. But we need learning, loving, missional communities to really grasp and memorize the Bible. Bible memorization transforms our lives and communities, especially when it's a group effort. Sure, personal Bible memorization that prioritizes insular, individualized, and personal piety is pretty effective for what it is; it creates people with an enormous sense of self-assurance. But we are interested in Bible memorization that leads people to discipleship and mission. Such transformative Bible memorization happens with others, in loving and supportive community, and with a view to joining with us in God's mission in the world. Relationships form us. They are pivotal to discipleship and Bible memory. They shape our outlook, priorities, values, beliefs, and habits. We learn and grow in community. We memorize and remember in community.

Years ago, when I (Michael) was doing my first degree in theology, I had enormous difficulty memorizing Greek vocabulary and declensions. If you don't know what Greek declensions are, look it up. It's as scary as it sounds. You couldn't complete New Testament studies if you didn't pass Greek, and I was floundering. That was, until a group of us decided to form a study group to memorize it together. We met in a dusty old storeroom in the college library and used a blackboard and flash cards to force ourselves to memorize it together. When one or another of us felt like giving up, the group dynamic motivated that person to stick with it. And it worked. We all passed Greek. (In my case, just.)

Studying how people learn in communities, Emily Lardner and Gillies Malnarich of the Washington Center at Evergreen State College say that learning with others can have a huge impact on us and what we retain and apply. They say that learning communities offer a great deal to their members, especially in today's world, including "curricular coherence; integrative, high-quality learning; collaborative knowledge-construction; and skills and knowledge relevant to living in a complex, messy, diverse world."[3]

Collaborative and relational learning is about learning things together. This involves friendship, mutuality, spurring each other on, and keeping each other accountable. Like my Greek study group. This can happen face-to-face (over coffee or lunch, in a classroom, or in a small group) or through online forums, chat rooms, Skype, and so on. The point is that we are learning and growing together. And we are doing it with a shared commitment to each other as disciples of Jesus Christ. At an earlier time in life, I (Graham) met weekly with a friend to memorize Bible verses. We memorized whole sections of the Bible, and I know that I would never have done it or memorized so much on my own.

So what does this look like? Find a friend who will memorize the Bible with you. Or start a group dedicated to memorizing the Bible and applying its commands and wisdom together. Meet regularly to memorize together. Keep each other accountable. Spur each other on. Encourage each other. Pray with each other as you press in on God to help you memorize the Bible and grow as world-changing disciples. Commit to learning and memorizing together. Practice together. Evaluate together. Apply together. Discuss insights together. As a result of what you are learning and memorizing, create new habits and ministries together. As you memorize Bible verses, seek to do so with others, in loving relationships, committed to growing as disciples and impacting the world together.

3. Linger: Form Habits as You Memorize

We remember what we learn through habits.

In the next chapter we will outline a suggested method for memorizing the verses we've provided. But let's take a moment to look at the habits of memory. A *habit* is an action done on a regular basis, often with the intent of making it a core and regular part of your life. It is a specific activity repeated constantly in order to build a skill.

Habits are about *lingering* with the texts and letting them go deep into your mind and heart. They include setting aside time each day to memorize (discipline), reviewing what you've memorized each day (active recall), doing lots of repetition (rote learning), and getting creative from time to time (e.g., using mnemonics, visualization, and dramatization). Let's briefly explore six core habits that aid memorization.

(a) Start planning. Have a set plan for how many verses you will memorize each week (we offer that plan in the next chapter). Then follow a regular, daily program of memorizing verses and revisiting ones you've already learned.

(b) Focus on vocal repetition. A key way to learn verses is just to repeat them every day. Spoken repetition is the best way to do this. Saying verses aloud embeds them in your memory. Repeat the Bible verse you are memorizing over and over. Include not just the words of the verse, but also the Bible reference. Repeat the verse, say, ten or twenty times during the day (checking you've got it right with a "verse card" in your pocket). Learn the verse word-perfectly.

(c) Use emphasis (dramatization). As you are memorizing a verse (speaking it aloud), emphasize one part of the verse. Next time, emphasize a different part. Then, emphasize a different part again. This changing of emphasis will help you remember the verse.

(d) Review over time. Go back often and review the verses you've already memorized by repeating them again. In the next chapter, we'll show how we've grouped verses around five topics (Bless, Eat, Listen, Learn, Sent—BELLS) to help you memorize through repetition, and review what you've learned.

(e) Look after yourself. Lots of studies show that you will remember more if you look after yourself. Exercise improves memory by improving cognitive performance on many levels. So does adequate sleep and a good diet. If you want to get really good at memorizing the Bible, then make sure you are exercising regularly, eating healthily, getting enough sleep, and finding ways to manage stress.

(f) Learn with a group or friend. As we mentioned earlier, meet with a group or with a friend who is also committed to learning Bible verses. Keep each other accountable. Test each other's learning. Make

this an encouraging moment. Set a time to meet weekly or once every two weeks, and test each other's learning, and offer loads of support and encouragement.

Okay, those six habits are essential. But here are three more optional habits that you might also find helpful:

(g) Try Christian meditation. Sit quietly in a peaceful spot for ten minutes, just focusing on breathing and quieting your heart and mind. Now, repeat the Bible verse you are learning aloud, over and over. Repeat the verse slowly and quietly and prayerfully. Let the verse sink deeply into your heart as you listen to its words and as you let it draw you into prayer.

(h) Try mnemonics. Mnemonics are imaginative devices for remembering things. Try them occasionally. There are many kinds of mnemonics, but the most common are acronyms, music jingles, or phrases. Here are some examples. BELLS is an acronym, or a *name mnemonic* (Bless, Eat, Listen, Learn, Sent). When children sing their ABC's, they are not only singing a jingle, they are using a *music mnemonic*. The phrase "Every good boy deserves fruit" (EGBDF) is a way of remembering the position of musical notes on the lines of the treble clef—a *word mnemonic*. These devices can be really helpful. If you want to quote seven key Bible verses from memory in a sermon on mission, for instance, you might link each verse to the letters MISSION.

(i) Try narratives. A compelling story line can help us remember a string of verses. Try to remember through stories from time to time. Ed Cooke, a grand master of memory, is the author of *Remember, Remember: Learn the Stuff You Thought You Never Could*. He is also a cofounder of Memrise, a free education program available online that offers learning techniques through memory skills. He says story lines can help you to memorize stuff. "Creating your own mnemonic

stories is as simple as it sounds. First, find an image you associate with each item. Second, link those images together into the most vivid narrative that you can imagine. Don't worry about what each thing should be represented by, just go with whatever comes to mind first: trust your imagination to do the work for you."[4] You can do this with complex stories or simple ones, depending on how much you want to memorize. If you want to remember John 3:16, for instance, you might imagine this story: Dozens of people from every nationality gather together in a field, to be swept up in God's loving arms ("God so loved the world"). As they are embraced by God, they look toward a distant hill and see Jesus on the cross ("that he gave his one and only Son"). They fall on their knees and worship Jesus ("that whoever believes in him"). On one side of the field is a raging fire, and on the other side a golden city. They stand and walk with God toward the golden city ("shall not perish but have eternal life"). This is just one example of how a simple story can help you remember the key parts of a verse or a series of verses in order.

In his book *Moonwalking with Einstein: The Art and Science of Remembering Everything*, Joshua Foer offers a series of tips and tricks for memorizing large amounts of information or bodies of text.[5] He says the secret is novelty. Use lots of different novel techniques. Link verses with lots of new and novel images and stories. Vary where you are memorizing, constantly. Keep things fresh, novel, new, and engaging. That's how we remember!

As you memorize Bible verses, form new habits. Linger with these verses, letting them penetrate deeply into your mind and heart and life.

4. Link: Make Creative Links as You Memorize

We remember what we learn through imaginative links.

We learn through our whole bodies and senses and beings. The Bible finds its way deep into our hearts not only through repetition but also through beauty, art, poetry, story, nature, and more. The voice of Jesus speaks to us through the Bible, but also through all the beauty and the suffering we see in the world. The two confirm and reinforce each other. This is about paying attention to what the Spirit is saying and doing in the world. How is the Spirit confirming his Word through beautiful artwork, novels, nature, poetry, music, architecture, and more? How is the Spirit inviting you to respond to his Word through what he is doing in society and in your neighborhood? How do contemporary events, the winds of social change, and the triumphs and sufferings of humanity confirm and fortify the biblical texts you are memorizing? What connections do you see between what God's Word says and what he is doing in the world today?

Whenever I (Graham) smell cut grass, I remember being a boy on my parents' property as my father worked on our lawn. When I hear the Wham! song "Careless Whisper," I remember going on vacations as a teenager to the north coast of Australia. When I hear the sound of cicadas on a hot Sydney summer day, I remember long walks around my grandparents' small farm as a child. And whenever I recite John 3:16, I remember, as a ten-year-old, walking a few blocks from my house to a weekly Bible study for children, where I sang and memorized Bible verses with my friends.

We often remember what we are memorizing when we link it to a meaningful person, scene, smell, event, or something else (like music, poetry, a movie, a sunset, the beach, and so on). We need to look for ways the links reinforce the importance and themes of these Bible texts and call us to personal growth, prayer, and action. This is about *listening* to what the Spirit is saying to you and how he is helping you make connections between these verses and your daily life.

Scientists have long known the power of emotions to form memories. When something impacts us emotionally, we remember it. Our autobiographical memories are usually filled with people, places, words, music, and events that affected us emotionally. Emotion affects what we prioritize, what we notice, what we store in our brains, and how we process, retrieve, and apply that information. So, associating Bible texts with things that stir great emotion in us can have a powerful effect on memory. When we link a Bible verse or passage with a glorious sunset, a painful heartache, a beautiful piece of music or artwork, a time of intense change, an experience of deep community, or a terrible injustice, then that biblical text can sink deeply into our hearts and minds.

Things have to impact us to lodge in our memories and hearts. We remember things that are emotional, unusual, salient, or shocking. This is often called the "Von Restorff effect" after the German psychiatrist and pediatrician Hedwig von Restorff. She proved that we more easily remember something when it is different or peculiar from the group of which it is part.

You can't manufacture emotion, but you can find creative ways to link biblical texts with the kind of emotionally impactful things we've described. Listen for the way art, beauty, nature, and public events resonate with certain Bible verses. See the way these underpin the significance of these Bible texts and call you to prayer and action. Link the Bible verses you are learning with themes in (and feelings and impressions you get from) stories, novels, art, poetry, nature, beauty, and current events. This is about listening to what the Spirit is saying to you and the connections he's making between these Bible verses and your life. We remember what we learn through imaginative links.

5. Live: Apply Your Learning as You Memorize

We remember what we apply and put into practice.

Shane Claiborne and Tony Campolo are friends of ours who are committed to peacemaking, justice, and mission. Shane has worked alongside Mother Teresa in Calcutta, spent time in Baghdad with the Iraq Peace Team, planted intentional communities, and served extensively in ministries of social justice, peacemaking, and community development. Tony has spent his life working for global and social justice, addressing issues like urban poverty, unbridled capitalism, militarized societies, and social and economic corruption. Together, Shane and Tony founded Red Letter Christians.

When you ask Shane Claiborne and Tony Campolo what makes them passionate for justice and discipleship, they tell you clearly—the words and life of Jesus. As they read the Bible, they are challenged by the radical life and message of Jesus, and they seek to live as his disciples. They are following after the radical faith and activist lifestyle modeled by Jesus in the Gospels.

> The goal . . . is simple: To take Jesus seriously by endeavoring to live out His radical, counter-cultural teachings as set forth in scripture, and especially embracing the lifestyle prescribed in the Sermon on the Mount. By calling ourselves Red Letter Christians, we refer to the fact that in many Bibles the words of Jesus are printed in red. We, therefore, assert that we are committed first and foremost to doing what Jesus said. Jesus calls us away from the consumerist values that dominate contemporary America. Instead, he calls us to meet the needs of the poor. He also calls us to be merciful, which has strong implications in terms of war and capital punishment. After all, when Jesus tells us to love our enemies, he probably means we shouldn't kill them.[6]

Shane and Tony aren't the only ones who tell stories of a shift from reading the Bible to applying it. When John Wimber, founder of the Vineyard, read in the Gospels about signs and wonders and about miraculous healings, casting out demons, and God's concern for the poor, he determined to do the things he was reading about. When Pete Greig read the Bible's commands to "pray without ceasing," he and a group of friends started what became the 24-7 Prayer Movement, inspiring a generation to put those words into action. When William Tyndale read the command to make disciples of all nations, he felt compelled that this would happen only if all people could read and interpret the Bible for themselves, leading him to translate the Bible into English.

What do we learn from people like Shane Claiborne, Tony Campolo, John Wimber, Pete Greig, William Tyndale, and so many others? The best way to learn the Bible and the way of Jesus—to get these deeply into our hearts and minds—is to live them out. When we follow the commands and wisdom of the Bible, we show that it is authoritative and compelling. We put our faith and our memorization into practice. We remember what we apply and put into practice because it costs us something. The verses are in our minds, they are changing our hearts, and they are leading us to imitate and follow Jesus Christ. The verses become a living and life-changing part of our lives. We show that this isn't just head knowledge; this is what we truly believe!

As you memorize Bible verses, apply what you are learning through courageous, prayerful, and compassionate action. Live the verses out in your personal discipleship and in your family, ministry, and neighborhood. Let the Bible draw you into a Christian life that seeks justice, mercy, peace, reconciliation, and change—both personally and within groups in your church and neighborhood. Apply the Bible verses you are learning as you pursue a life shaped around the prophetic words of Jesus and Scripture. This is about living as disciples and followers of the Jesus way. We remember what we apply and put into practice.

6. Lean: Lean on the Spirit's Inspiration as You Memorize

We remember what inspires us
and what the Spirit empowers us to recall.

Helen Keller was a deaf, blind Christian leader and author who campaigned for women's suffrage, labor rights, rights for people with disabilities, pacifism, antimilitarism, and a wide range of other causes. She is often remembered as an extraordinary political activist. She traveled to over forty countries championing human rights, pacifism, birth control, and women's suffrage, and was often attacked for her radical, countercultural views.

In her autobiography *Midstream*, Keller describes how she leaned on the Spirit during times of profound struggle in her ministry and her fight for social justice. The words of the Bible fired her up for God's justice and mercy, and the Spirit put her heart and mind at rest through the words of Scripture. She writes,

> I have read and reread it until in many parts the pages have faded out—I mean, my fingers have rubbed off the dots, and I must supply whole verses from memory, especially the Psalms, the Prophets, and the Gospels. To the Bible I always go for confidence when waves of doubt rush over me and no voice is near to reassure me.[7]

As she leaned on the Spirit, he brought the words of the Bible to her, and this filled her with fresh confidence, courage, and comfort.

Do you lack courage? Do you need comfort? Do you long for guidance? Are you unsure whether you can memorize the Bible? The answer is leaning on the Spirit's inspiration and empowerment. The Spirit will make you brave and give you comfort. The Spirit will help you memorize and recall the Bible.

As you memorize Bible verses, humbly lean on the Spirit's power and presence. Jesus will help you recall the verses and live them out for the sake of his mission and Kingdom and for the Father's glory. Ask the Holy Spirit to inspire you with these verses. Invite him to cause these verses to fill and enthuse your heart and mind and lead you into a weird, radical, world-changing discipleship.

Releasing the Radical Mind and Life

We've tried to show that the art of memory can be a dynamic and creative endeavor. And we think the tools we've outlined above will add significantly to the success of your journey in Bible memorization. But we'd be remiss if we didn't say in all honesty that sometimes memorization can be tedious and mundane as well. While it can be a joy, it also involves good old-fashioned hard work.

Recently, I (Michael) was reading a magazine interview with the Italian opera singer Andrea Bocelli, in which he was asked what the young version of himself would think of the now sixty-year-old man he'd become. He answered,

> As a young boy I was agnostic. The young Andrea would probably not understand that today I believe in faith and great values, in the need to be pious every day. Over the years I have come to believe that faith cannot be acquired effortlessly: just as any other discipline, it requires commitment, perseverance and sacrifice. To be committed to faith, means we need to comply with simple deeds that may even appear tedious.[8]

Spoken like a true virtuoso singer, a man who has practiced scales all his life. Singing teacher Jeannette Lovetri says, "It takes about 10 years to be a master singer. Ten years of study, investigation, involvement, experience, experiment, exploration, and development, and in some way, that's when you start really being an artist."[9] Bocelli knows this, and he knows that the life of faith requires similar devotion to those simple deeds that can appear tedious. Bible memorization is just such a deed.

The science of memorization is fascinating; the art of memorizing is inspiring and a lifelong pursuit. The words of the Bible will transform your life, if you let them. Celebrate the process. As you memorize the Bible, enjoy your learning, your deepening friendships, your fresh expressions of peacemaking and justice seeking and reconciliation, and your achievements. Bible memorization has the potential to launch you into a transforming, missional, and world-changing lifestyle and discipleship.

4

the memory system

We are what we repeatedly do.
Excellence, then, is not an act, but a habit.

ARISTOTLE

There's no such thing as safe or tame discipleship. Discipleship is always dangerous and risky and countercultural. The Kingdom ethics and gospel message of Jesus confront the powers and principalities of this world. Jesus calls his disciples to show a different way in the world—an alternative to racism, sexism, fear, conflict, and so on. So if your reading of Scripture doesn't put you in harm's way, you're not reading it right.

Dallas Willard says that one of the best ways to get this vision for discipleship to soak into your heart—and to seek a spiritual life that reflects the heart of Jesus—is to memorize Scripture. Memorizing the Bible can fill our hearts and minds with the transforming, world-changing message of our God. Memorizing can help us live as disciples, living in ways that reflect the Sermon on the Mount and the Beatitudes. As Willard says, "Bible memorization is absolutely fundamental to spiritual formation. . . . This book of the law shall not depart out of your mouth. That's where you need it! How does it get in your mouth? Memorization."[1]

We need a good method to memorize well. In this chapter, we outline the method of our Kingdom Impact Memory System (KIMS). We'll organize the passages in our system using the acronym BELLS because our approach is shaped around the five habits in Michael's earlier book *Surprise the World*—Bless, Eat, Listen, Learn, and Sent. In addition to the basic set of verses, in appendix 2 we offer a strategy for memorizing the Sermon on the Mount (Matthew 5–7) in twenty-four or forty-eight months, for those who want to challenge themselves further.

The Forerunners of KIMS

The Kingdom Impact Memory System (KIMS) is designed to complement the Topical Memory System (TMS), initially developed by Dawson Trotman, founder of The Navigators. Trotman was a real stickler for Bible memorization. In 1928, just two years after becoming a Christian, he had identified eighty-five Scripture verses that he thought every believer should know by heart. He began commending this system to students at Biola. In 1935, he expanded the number of verses to 105, broken into thirty-five topics with three verses for each topic. During the Second World War, Navigators serving in the armed forces carried these verses all around the world. Soon, people in England and Belgium and Germany were signing up to join the program.

The popularity of Trotman's program led The Navigators to get even more serious about Scripture memory. In 1943, they undertook a complete overhaul of the study method, getting expert advice from biblical scholars and renaming and repackaging Dawson's program as the Topical Memory System. By the late 1950s, tens of thousands of people had enrolled in the course.

Later The Navigators decided to reduce the number of verses in the course from 108 to 60. Further revisions occurred in 1965, 1969, and 1975 in order to make the program as user-friendly as possible. More recently, an app for smartphones has been created to supplement the old card system.[2]

We love the TMS. Not long after I (Michael) became a Christian, I undertook a Navigators discipleship course and was infected with the TMS bug, carrying cards with me everywhere and memorizing as many verses as I could. As we and others have noted, the TMS does focus principally on verses that emphasize personal salvation, assurance of faith, and victory over sin. So while the TMS is our forerunner and a wonderful companion to our program, we have designed KIMS to broaden your appreciation of the big, expansive gospel we discussed in chapter 2, including justice seeking, peacemaking, and faith sharing.

Another forerunner to KIMS is, as we've mentioned, Michael's book *Surprise the World*. We recommend you read this book while you're learning these Bible verses. It will give you a context and framework for the BELLS model—Bless, Eat, Listen, Learn, and Sent—which informs our selection of Bible verses.[3]

The Goals of KIMS

The Kingdom Impact Memory System is designed to help you learn five things:

1. To memorize the Bible
2. To apply the verses you are memorizing
3. To recall and review the verses you've memorized
4. To develop lifelong habits of Bible memorization
5. To learn Bible verses that help you live a "questionable" life that's generous, hospitable, Spirit-led, Christlike, and missionary

The KIMS Topics and Verses

There are five topics in KIMS, based on the five habits in *Surprise the World*. Each topic then has four subtopics with two verses each. That's eight verses per topic to memorize, a total of forty verses in all.

Topics are important because they help you understand the meaning and importance of the verses you are learning. They will also help you link the verses you are learning with each of the five habits of highly missional people:

1. Blessing people, both inside and outside the church,
2. Eating together, by sharing meals with believers and nonbelievers alike,
3. Listening to the guidance and direction of the Holy Spirit as we engage with those around us,
4. Learning Christ as our leader and model for making disciples, and
5. seeing ourselves as Sent by God to anywhere life takes us

I (Michael) describe the value of the BELLS topics and habits this way:

> [BELLS offers] a simple, easy-to-adopt set of habits that do unleash essential missional values: engagement with neighbors, connection with each other, a deeper experience of God's leading, a stronger understanding of the gospel, and a framework for identifying ourselves as missionaries. . . . I'm not suggesting that BELLS is a magic bullet or anything like that. But it is a really handy tool for mobilizing Christians up, in, and out into mission. That is, *up* into deeper connection with the Triune God; *in* to a stronger sense of community with other believers; and *out* into the neighborhood.[4]

Here is the KIMS system for how the topics, subtopics, verses, and weekly schedule relate:

- There are five topics and twenty subtopics (see list below).
- There are forty verses in total (that's two verses per subtopic).
- You will learn two verses per week over twenty weeks (that's one week in each subtopic).

TOPIC 1: BLESS

Subtopic 1.1: Affirm and Honor Others
1 Thessalonians 5:11; Galatians 3:26-28

Subtopic 1.2: Release Finances
Matthew 6:19-21, 24; Matthew 6:2-4

Subtopic 1.3: Exhibit Practical Giving
1 John 3:17-18; 2 Corinthians 8:7

Subtopic 1.4: Commit to Prayer
1 Timothy 2:1-2; Jeremiah 29:7

TOPIC 2: EAT

Subtopic 2.1: Welcome Refugees and Immigrants
Matthew 25:35-36, 40; Deuteronomy 10:18-19

Subtopic 2.2: Show Hospitality and Welcome
Luke 14:13-14; Hebrews 13:2

Subtopic 2.3: Enjoy Table Fellowship
Luke 7:34-35; Luke 24:30-31

Subtopic 2.4: Show Justice, Mercy, Compassion
Zechariah 7:9-10; James 2:15-17

TOPIC 3: LISTEN

Subtopic 3.1: Repent and Lament
Acts 3:19-20; Joel 2:12-13

Subtopic 3.2: Be Peacemakers
Matthew 5:9; Romans 12:14, 18

Subtopic 3.3: Seek Guidance and Direction
Psalm 25:4-5; Proverbs 2:6-9

Subtopic 3.4: Be Disciplined and Corrected
Hebrews 12:7-8, 11; Revelation 3:19

TOPIC 4: LEARN

Subtopic 4.1: Love God, Neighbors, and Enemies
Mark 12:29-31; Matthew 5:43-46

Subtopic 4.2: Seek Reconciliation
2 Corinthians 5:18; Colossians 1:19-20

Subtopic 4.3: Display Humility and Self-Sacrifice
Philippians 2:3-4; Matthew 16:24-25

Subtopic 4.4: Proclaim Freedom and Gospel
Luke 4:18-19; Romans 1:16-17

TOPIC 5: SENT

Subtopic 5.1: Be a Sent Community
Matthew 28:18-20; Acts 1:8

Subtopic 5.2: Pursue Justice
Micah 6:8; Isaiah 58:6-7

Subtopic 5.3: Be Incarnational and Present
John 20:21; Amos 5:24

Subtopic 5.4: Keep Christianity Weird
1 Peter 2:9; Romans 12:1-2

The Tools of KIMS

To ensure greater success in your journey of memorization, we have created tools to support you.

Chapter 5 of this book is the *memorizing workbook*. It recaps the method of memorization in a functional way so you are sure of what you're doing with these verses every week. It will give you:

- a verse checklist (forty verses, grouped in the five topics)
- a weekly memorizing schedule (twenty weeks)
- a verse review list (with all forty verses listed in the order they appear in the Bible)
- questions for meditation and group reflection
- individual and group challenges for you to apply
- some sample prayers

The *memory verses* are bound together in pages in this book.

The Techniques of KIMS

Here are the key techniques you should use as you memorize the Bible. You'll want to refer to this list often in the coming weeks. We think you'll be surprised and delighted by how much you will memorize!

One: Focus on the Essential Principles

There are some basic, commonly understood principles for Bible memory. Two of the most essential are:

- *Consistently* memorize verses every week. You have two verses per week to memorize—make memorizing them a priority.
- *Set aside time every day* to memorize verses and to review the Bible verses you've already memorized.

We've added a third:

- *Find someone who will memorize with you.* It may be one person, or it may be a group. Test each other's learning, and hold each other accountable.

If you find you haven't quite learned the verses one week, keep moving forward. Keep working on the verses you're struggling with even as you get started on the next week. If you pause in your progress, you'll stop your momentum and may be tempted to give up. It's much better to put in extra effort to learn the verses you're struggling with word-perfectly, while also doing the same for the verses of the week you're in. A recent university study showed that on average it takes two months for people to form new habits.[5] For some people, it can take up to eight months! So it may take a while, but you will form the habit if you persist.

Two: Find Ways to Keep Bible Memorizing Fresh

There are ways to keep memorizing fresh. These include occasionally using narratives and mnemonics to memorize (see previous chapter). Also use the *Questions* we have provided for meditation and group reflection, the *Challenges* we have provided for you to apply individually and in groups, and the *Prayers* we have provided. All of these things will help keep your Bible memorizing fresh.

Three: Learn the Topic, the Reference, and the Verse

When memorizing verses, it's important to memorize the topic and reference number too. I (Graham) learned this lesson early on when I was learning the verses of The Navigators' *Topical Memory System*. I love learning words; I don't like remembering numbers! So I'd memorize the words of a verse but be a little halfhearted about learning the reference. I quickly discovered that quoting a verse is not helpful if you can't remember where it comes from!

So here's what you should do. As you memorize, say each part in this order:

- the topic
- the reference
- the verse
- the reference
- the topic

Before you know it, you'll know the verse word-perfectly, including the reference and the topic. Believe us, it works!

Four: Choose the Best Time and Place to Memorize

What's the best time and place to memorize? The key is finding *a time that works* for you, and a time and place that's *free of distractions*.

When I (Graham) first started memorizing the Bible, I tried doing it at night. But I found that by the evening I was too tired, and the busyness of the day or the evening interrupted my good plans or squeezed Bible memorizing out altogether. So I decided to combine Bible memorizing with my morning walk. I get up in the morning and walk for thirty minutes. I started using that walk to memorize the verses for the week and to review the verses I had already learned. I chose a quiet park, free from distractions. If I played music in my earbuds while walking, I always made sure it was instrumental so that I could focus on the words in the memory verse. Combining my morning walk with Bible memorizing works for me! It combines my best time with my best place. It gets me memorizing early in the day, making it a priority for me.

Some people find that the best two times of the day are just before they go to bed at night and also first thing in the morning. You might also look for spare times during the day to review and practice. The keys are: choose a regular *daily* time and place, find a place *free of distractions*, and make learning and reviewing *a priority*.

Five: Learn Word-Perfectly through Memory Drilling

Learning the verses word-perfectly helps cement them in your memory. Learning word-perfectly aids memory, helps with reviewing what you've learned, and builds your confidence that you can memorize. The Kingdom Impact Memory System offers our verses in various Bible translations. Choose one translation and stick with it for all the verses you memorize.

Memory specialists talk about "megadrilling" as a way of making the most of the power of repetition.[6] Here's how "megadrilling" works:

- *Repeat, repeat, repeat.* Say the verse over and over (around fifteen times), until you know it. Some people find it useful to write the verse down as they're saying it (do this if it helps), checking to see if they've got it right.

- *Use active recall.* Recall the verse around thirty times during the day. Memory studies have shown that recalling a memory (like a name, a formula, or a text) thirty times is especially powerful for cementing it in your memory.

- *Ask a friend.* Invite a friend to test whether you've memorized the verse. Get them to test that you know the topic, the reference, and the verse.

Six: Work through the Topics Using the Weekly Schedule

You will learn the forty verses over twenty weeks (two verses per week). That means you're spending four weeks on the topic Bless, four weeks on Eat, and so on. This moves you through the verses and topics systematically. It also gives you a helpful memory program to follow.

You'll see in the next chapter that each week offers the following plan:

1. The Topic
2. The Two Verses
3. Your Plan for the Week
4. Questions for Meditation and Group Reflection
5. Challenges for You to Apply Individually and in Groups
6. Sample Prayers

Following the weekly schedule keeps you moving forward with your Bible memory. It builds your Bible memory and knowledge over the weeks and keeps you focused on the five core topics. And it builds your confidence as you go.

Seven: Follow These Hints and Tips

Here are some principles for memorizing the Bible. They will help you as you start learning a verse, while you're learning it, and when you're reviewing what you've learned.[7]

AS YOU START MEMORIZING A VERSE . . .

- *Follow the schedule.* It's important to follow the weekly schedule, so choose the verse you're up to.

- *Pray.* Pray for God's empowering presence to help you learn and remember the verse.

- *Read and reflect.* Read the verse through once slowly, listening closely to the words. Read the verse in the context of the Bible passage it is in. Ask yourself some questions: What does this verse and passage say? What does this mean? How might these words impact my life and change my church, neighborhood, family, and society? Why are these words important? Now, stop and pray through these thoughts and reflections.

- *Notice the topic.* Notice which BELLS topic and subtopic the verse relates to. Ask yourself why you think this verse is connected with this specific BELLS topic (i.e., Bless, Eat, Listen, Learn, Sent).

- *Schedule time.* Now, make sure you've set aside time in your day and week to memorize this week's verses and to review what you've learned.

WHILE YOU'RE LEARNING THE VERSE . . .

- *Print a copy of the verse.* Make sure you have it with you at all times (or close at hand).

- *Follow this order.* As you memorize, say each part in this order: *the topic, the reference, the verse, the reference, the topic.* This will help cement the topic, reference, and verse in your mind and heart.

- *Learn through phrases.* The writers of the *Topical Memory System* lay out this step well: "After learning the topic and reference, learn the first phrase of the verse. Once you have learned the topic, reference, and first phrase and have repeated them several times, continue adding more phrases after you can quote correctly what you have already learned."[8]

- *Repeat aloud and often.* Say the verse over and over (around fifteen times), until you know it. Try writing the verse down as you're saying it, as this can help. Keep checking to make sure you've got it right.

- *Use active recall.* Recall the verse around thirty times during the day, testing your recall.

- *Ask a friend to lend a hand.* Invite a friend to test whether you've memorized the verse. Get them to test whether you know the topic, the reference, and the verse. If you are part of a weekly small group, you might also use some of your meeting time to test each other's recall of the verses.

- *Pray.* Keep praying throughout the day that God will lodge the verse in your heart and mind and also lead you to change and grow in mission, discipleship, and ministry as a result of learning this verse.

- *Use the Questions.* Use the questions for meditation and group reflection.

- *Use the Challenges.* Try the challenges for individuals and groups.

- *Use the Prayers.* Spend time praying the sample prayers or writing and/or praying your own.

AFTER YOU'VE LEARNED THE VERSE . . .

- *Review often.* Set aside regular, daily time to review the verses you've learned.

- *Speak.* We find it helps to say the verses in conversations, sermons, witnessing, small group times, college lessons, and teaching sessions. Saying the verses you've learned often and aloud (and showing you know the meaning and context and applications) can really help solidify your learning and recall.

- *Apply.* Keep looking for creative and missional ways to apply the verses you've learned in your own life and with a sent community.

- *Final tip.* Again from the writers of the *Topical Memory System*: "Review the verse immediately after learning it, and repeat it frequently in the next few days. This is crucial for getting the verse firmly fixed in mind because of how quickly we tend to forget something recently learned. REVIEW! REVIEW! REVIEW! Repetition is the best way to engrave the verses on your memory."[9]

Eight: Keep Learning and Reviewing

Nothing beats reviewing to cement and engrave Scripture verses in your memory. Review the verses you've learned often, preferably in a group or with a friend. In chapter 5, we've provided a verse review list to help you as you review (with all forty verses listed in the order they appear in the Bible).

But what happens when you've learned all sixty verses of The Navigator's Topical Memory System and all forty verses of the Kingdom Impact Memory System? Keep learning more! The five BELLS topics will help you to do this. Look for Bible passages that speak to the themes of being generous, hospitable, Spirit-led, Christlike, and missionary, and keep adding more and more verses to your list of those to memorize. Set a goal of learning one or two new verses every week. See appendix 3, "My Personal Collection of Memory Verses," where you can start gathering your own collection of new memory verses.

Nine: Use the Questions, Challenges, and Prayers

Bible memorizing can sometimes become too intellectual and individualistic. We've added *Questions, Challenges,* and *Prayers* to each of the twenty weeks to help your Bible memorizing become meaningful, relational, missional, and prayerful. The *Questions*, *Challenges*, and *Prayers* can be used individually. They can really help you grow spiritually when used this way. But they are even better when they are used in a group.

The Relationships and Lifestyle of the Kingdom Impact Memory System

As we suggested in the previous chapter, loving and supportive relationships are the key to learning, spiritual formation, and mission. Our weekly *Questions*, *Challenges*, and *Prayers* will help you develop deep relationships while you memorize the Bible.

We strongly encourage you to memorize with a friend or with a supportive group. The group might be a Bible study group, a missional action team, a neighborhood group, a ministry team, a group of colleagues or peers, a college or university class, your family, a small group of accountability peers, or something similar.

The weekly *Questions*, *Challenges*, and *Prayers* help you develop your relationship with God and others. This way you can love people and lean on God while you learn the Bible and live it out in world-changing ways. We don't offer many ministry and missional challenges for you to try—just a few to get you started, to help you apply the verses you are learning, personally and in groups. You will most likely adapt these to suit your context, or even add your own.

The *Challenges* include such things as:

- *Bless:* I will bless three people this week, at least one of whom is not a member of our church.
- *Eat:* I will eat with three people this week, at least one of whom is not a member of our church.
- *Listen:* I will spend at least one period of the week listening for the Spirit's voice.
- *Learn:* I will spend at least one period of the week learning Christ.

- *Sent:* I will journal throughout the week about all the ways I alerted others to the universal reign of God through Christ.[10]

These *Challenges* are just suggestions for how you might apply the verses you are memorizing in ways that witness to the gospel of Jesus Christ. Build on them and add to them as you seek ways to live out these verses in your life, church, and neighborhood.

A Memory System That Empowers and Deepens Your Discipleship

Through the words of the Bible, Jesus invites us to pursue deeper discipleship, within sent communities, in local neighborhoods. The forty verses you'll memorize will empower you to live a life that impacts the world. They'll also increase your desire to hear the Spirit speaking to you through the whole story line of the Bible, calling you to live out the justice and peace and reconciliation of Jesus Christ.

As we write this, our country of Australia is awarding honors to those who've served our country in our military, educational, health, social, and civil institutions. We don't want to take away from the contributions of these people at all, but most of us won't be celebrated in such public ways, which can make us start to think that changing the world is beyond our reach, which can then discourage us from action—even give us an excuse not to act. But be encouraged: The world is changed by the quiet, unnoticed actions of each one of us. And when our actions are aligned with God's Kingdom values, the world can't help but be changed by them. As Paul says,

God chose the foolish things of the world to shame the wise;
God chose the weak things of the world to shame the strong.
God chose the lowly things of this world and the despised
things—and the things that are not—to nullify the things
that are, so that no one may boast before him. It is because

of him that you are in Christ Jesus, who has become for us wisdom from God—that is, our righteousness, holiness and redemption.

1 CORINTHIANS 1:27-30

Disciples who are seeking to bring justice, healing, and reconciliation don't usually live loud and showy lives. Sometimes we get noticed, but most often we don't. This kind of discipleship is lived out among those who are working tirelessly as unheralded agents of reconciliation, prophets of justice, and people of peace. Their hearts and minds have been captivated and captured by the words of God, offered to us in the pages of the Bible.

Over and over again the voice of God comes to us through the words of the Bible, calling us to love reconciliation, to seek justice, and to promote peace. And when these words soak deeply into our minds and hearts, we are forever changed, as are the lives we touch.

Let justice roll on like a river,
    righteousness like a never-failing stream!

AMOS 5:24

He has shown you, O mortal, what is good.
    And what does the LORD require of you?
To act justly and to love mercy
    and to walk humbly with your God.

MICAH 6:8

the memory verses

*We are creatures of habit. . . . God knows this (since he created us),
and thus our gracious, redeeming God meets us where we are
by giving us Spirit-empowered, heart-calibrating, habit-forming
practices to retrain our loves. This is the means of the Spirit's
transformation, not an alternative to Spirit-shaped sanctification.
If we don't take this seriously, we will, in effect, be giving ourselves
over to all of the rival habit-forming practices of our culture.*

JAMES K. A. SMITH

Okay, here goes. In this chapter we provide you with the memory verses
you will learn. This chapter is, in effect, your memorizing workbook. It
recaps the method of memorization in a functional way, so you are sure
of what you're doing with these verses every week.

In this chapter you will find:

- verse checklists (forty selections of verses, grouped in the five
  topics)
- a weekly memorizing schedule (a plan for each of the twenty
  weeks)
- a verse review list (with all forty selections of verses listed in the
  order they appear in the Bible)
- questions for meditation and group reflection (for each week/
  subtopic)

- challenges for you to apply individually and in groups (for each week/subtopic)
- some sample prayers (for each week/subtopic)

A Brief Recap of How to Learn These Verses

Return to chapter 4 regularly to remind yourself of the best ways to memorize the Bible. Also refer to the nine habits of memorization described in chapter 3 (under "Linger"). Here are the key things to remember as you learn these verses:

- *Make a commitment* to learn the forty selections of verses over twenty weeks. That means you're spending four weeks on the topic Bless, four weeks on Eat, and so on.

- *Follow the weekly schedule.* This keeps you moving forward with your Bible memory. It builds your Bible memory and knowledge over the weeks and keeps you focused on the five core topics. And it builds your confidence as you go.

- *Consistently memorize* verses every week. You have two selections of verses per week to memorize—make memorizing them a priority.

- *Set aside time every day* to memorize verses, and to review the Bible verses you've already memorized.

- *Find someone who will memorize with you.* It may be one person or it may be a group. Test each other's learning and hold each other accountable.

- *Repeat, repeat, repeat.* Say the verse over and over (around fifteen times) until you know it. Keep checking to make sure you've got it right.

- *Use active recall.* Recall the verse around thirty times during the day.

- *Follow our hints and tips* as you memorize. See the list in chapter 4.

- *Use the weekly Questions, Challenges, and Prayers.* These can be used individually but are best used in a group. They will enliven and deepen your Bible memorizing. You may even like to read through the optional (but encouraged) "Recommended Readings" offered in appendix 4.

- *Keep the goals in mind and enjoy your learning!* The goals are to deepen your spiritual life, empower and deepen your discipleship, and help you learn and apply the five habits of highly missional people. Enjoy your learning! God is going to do incredible things in and through you as the words and message of the Bible transform your heart, mind, and life.

The Verses

In the back of this book you'll find the forty Bible verses in our Kingdom Impact Memory System (KIMS) printed on tear-off cards in four versions of the Bible: the New International Version (NIV), *The Message* (MSG), the English Standard Version (ESV), and the New Living Translation (NLT).

Habit	Topic	Memory Verse 1	Memory Verse 2
Bless Generosity	Affirm and Honor Others	1 Thessalonians 5:11	Galatians 3:26-28
	Release Finances	Matthew 6:19-21, 24	Matthew 6:2-4
	Exhibit Practical Giving	1 John 3:17-18	2 Corinthians 8:7
	Commit to Prayer	1 Timothy 2:1-2	Jeremiah 29:7

Habit	Topic	Memory Verse 1	Memory Verse 2
Eat *Hospitality*	Welcome Refugees and Immigrants	Matthew 25:35-36, 40	Deuteronomy 10:18-19
	Show Hospitality and Welcome	Luke 14:13-14	Hebrews 13:2
	Enjoy Table Fellowship	Luke 7:34-35	Luke 24:30-31
	Show Justice, Mercy, Compassion	Zechariah 7:9-10	James 2:15-17
Listen *Spirit-Led*	Repent and Lament	Acts 3:19-20	Joel 2:12-13
	Be Peacemakers	Matthew 5:9	Romans 12:14, 18
	Seek Guidance and Direction	Psalm 25:4-5	Proverbs 2:6-9
	Be Disciplined and Corrected	Hebrews 12:7-8, 11	Revelation 3:19
Learn *Christlike*	Love God, Neighbors, and Enemies	Mark 12:30-31	Matthew 5:43-46
	Seek Reconciliation	2 Corinthians 5:18	Colossians 1:19-20
	Display Humility and Self-Sacrifice	Philippians 2:3-4	Matthew 16:24-25
	Proclaim Freedom and Gospel	Luke 4:18-19	Romans 1:16-17
Sent *Missionary*	Be a Sent Community	Matthew 28:18-20	Acts 1:8
	Pursue Justice	Micah 6:8	Isaiah 58:6-7
	Be Incarnational and Present	John 20:21	Amos 5:24
	Keep Christianity Weird	1 Peter 2:9	Romans 12:1-2

These verses have been chosen because they inspire us to be a generous, hospitable, Spirit-led, Christlike, and missionary people. Scripture memorization (and particularly these passages) can help us to effectively and sustainably proclaim and demonstrate the universal rule and reign of Jesus Christ, living into the mission of God in our everyday lives. And once you've memorized these forty verses, you can keep going on memorizing the Bible, building a deep and Christlike faith.

To help you with reviewing what you've memorized, here we list all forty selections of verses in the order they appear in the Bible:

Old Testament	Gospels	Acts and Letters
Deuteronomy 10:18-19	Matthew 5:9	Acts 1:8
Psalm 25:4-5	Matthew 5:43-46	Acts 3:19-20
Proverbs 2:6-9	Matthew 6:2-4	Romans 1:16-17
Isaiah 58:6-7	Matthew 6:19-21, 24	Romans 12:1-2
Jeremiah 29:7	Matthew 16:24-25	Romans 12:14, 18
Joel 2:12-13	Matthew 25:35-36, 40	2 Corinthians 5:18
Amos 5:24	Matthew 28:18-20	2 Corinthians 8:7
Micah 6:8	Mark 12:30-31	Galatians 3:26-28
Zechariah 7:9-10	Luke 4:18-19	Philippians 2:3-4
	Luke 7:34-35	Colossians 1:19-20
	Luke 14:13-14	1 Thessalonians 5:11
	Luke 24:30-31	1 Timothy 2:1-2
	John 20:21	Hebrews 12:7-8, 11
		Hebrews 13:2
		James 2:15-17
		1 Peter 2:9
		1 John 3:17-18
		Revelation 3:1

For each of the twenty weeks of the Kingdom Impact Memory System (KIMS), we offer a brief paragraph of introduction to the verses you're memorizing. The verses, questions, challenges, prayers, and recommended readings that follow work together to help you understand and practice each week's central theme. The verses aren't progressive—they're not designed to build on the previous ones. Instead, they are chosen because they are individually reflective of the week's overarching theme. They each empower radical faith, activist spirituality, and missional community.

An important note: Most of these verses are directed to us as churches and groups, and not to us as individuals (*y'all* versus *you*). One function of KIMS is to offer a corrective to hyper-individualized readings of the Scriptures. Most of the verses, questions, reflections, and practices should thus be read as directed toward groups and not individuals. Please keep that in mind! We will regularly point out the *y'all* in these verses as a self-check for the reader (noticing how biased we can be toward the individualized reading).

Habit 1: Bless (Generosity)

We bless people, both inside and outside the church.

The first habit is blessing others. We'd like you to bless three people each week—at least one of whom is a member of your church and at least one of whom is *not*. In *Surprise the World*, I (Michael) say that this habit is about being generous. I describe how we bless others through words of affirmation, acts of kindness, and the giving of gifts. "We need to develop a rhythm of gift giving, time spending, and affirmation sharing as an end in itself because it fosters a spirit of generosity, it mirrors the character of God, and it alerts others to his reign."[1]

Check the box next to each verse after you've memorized it:

Affirm and Honor Others
☐ 1 Thessalonians 5:11
☐ Galatians 3:26-28

Release Finances
☐ Matthew 6:19-21, 24
☐ Matthew 6:2-4

Exhibit Practical Giving
☐ 1 John 3:17-18
☐ 2 Corinthians 8:7

Commit to Prayer
☐ 1 Timothy 2:1-2
☐ Jeremiah 29:7

WEEK 1

Topic: Bless (Generosity)
Subtopic: Affirm and Honor Others
Verses: 1 Thessalonians 5:11 and Galatians 3:26-28

Blessing others often involves affirming and honoring them. In 1 Thessalonians, Paul says the return of Jesus is near. Therefore, be sober, and be filled with faith, hope, and love. And "encourage one another and build each other up, just as in fact you are doing" (1 Thessalonians 5:11).

In Galatians 3:26-28, Paul says we are to honor each other in Christ, since we are all one in him. The old divisions of gender, race, class, wealth, and status must be set aside, since we are one in Christ, and we belong to him, and are now, together, Abraham's seed and heirs according to God's promise. Division is replaced with unity, and disrespect with honor. Bless people through words of affirmation, honor, and encouragement.

YOUR PLAN THIS WEEK

- Reread chapter 4 of this book to refresh your memory about how to memorize the Bible.

- Use Monday to read 1 Thessalonians 5:11 and Galatians 3:26-28 in their context. Reflect on their meaning in context and how to live them out in your life, church, and neighborhood. Notice that both these passages are directed toward groups and their collective actions, not just individuals.

- Use Tuesday and Wednesday to memorize 1 Thessalonians 5:11, and use Thursday and Friday to memorize Galatians 3:26-28. Use the weekend to practice both passages and to reflect on them.

- Mark off the verses on the checklist once you've learned them.

- Work through the *Questions*, *Challenges*, and *Prayer* given below, alone or in a group. Modify them or add to them as you feel led by the Spirit.

QUESTIONS FOR MEDITATION AND GROUP REFLECTION

- Who will you bless this week? Name at least one person in your church and one person outside your church.
- What kinds of things bless you? Why do they bless you?
- How can you get better at learning what blesses, encourages, and builds others up (1 Thessalonians 5:11)?
- How does seeing people as God's children affect the honor you give them? How can your church honor all people and their gifts to the whole church (regardless of race, ethnicity, gender, education, class, etc.) since we are now "one in Christ Jesus" (Galatians 3:26-28)?

CHALLENGES FOR YOU TO APPLY INDIVIDUALLY AND IN GROUPS

- Bless three people this week—at least one of whom is not a member of your church.
- Write a short letter of affirmation to someone this week, and send it to them.
- Memorize 1 Thessalonians 5:11 and Galatians 3:26-28.

A SAMPLE PRAYER

Open our hearts to our neighbors. May they become our friends.

Open our lives to strangers, immigrants, and those we don't yet know. Help us show welcome and embrace.

Open our tables, so they become places of friendship, community, and love.

Open our homes and our finances, so they bless others and express generosity.

Open our mouths to bless, affirm, and honor others. Lead us to live lives that affirm and honor others, building them up.

Give us the grace to be open, welcoming, affirming, and generous.

Amen.

WEEK 2

Topic: Bless (Generosity)
Subtopic: Release Finances
Verses: Matthew 6:19-21, 24 and Matthew 6:2-4

We bless others through our generosity and our transformed attitude toward money. Our heart and worship belong now to God, not money. We are devoted to God and serve him now, not money or possessions

(Matthew 6:19-21, 24). We choose to be a generous people who give to the needy—not in a showy way, but in a private and secret way, since our only desire is to bless others and glorify God (Matthew 6:2-4). Bless others through the way you and your group are generous with your money.

YOUR PLAN THIS WEEK

- Use Monday to read Matthew 6:19-21, 24 and Matthew 6:2-4 in their context. Reflect on their meaning in context and how to live them out in your life, church, and neighborhood. Notice that both these passages are directed toward groups and their collective actions, not just individuals.

- Use Tuesday and Wednesday to memorize Matthew 6:19-21, 24, and use Thursday and Friday to memorize Matthew 6:2-4. Use the weekend to practice the verses and to reflect on them.

- Take fifteen to twenty minutes each day to review the verses you've already learned. You may choose to write them down from memory. This will help ensure you don't forget them.

- Mark off the verses in the checklist once you've learned them.

- Work through the *Questions*, *Challenges*, and *Prayer* given below, alone or in a group. Modify them or add to them as you feel led by the Spirit.

QUESTIONS FOR MEDITATION AND GROUP REFLECTION

- Who will you bless this week? Name at least one person in your church and one person outside your church.
- Where is your heart and your treasure? How are you choosing to store up treasures in heaven? How is this reflected in your decisions, priorities, and actions (Matthew 6:19-21, 24)?

- How will you bless and give to the needy in secret this week (Matthew 6:2-4)?
- What are practical ways we can release finances personally and together, especially for the sake of the poor and the needy?

CHALLENGES FOR YOU TO APPLY INDIVIDUALLY AND IN GROUPS

- Bless three people this week—at least one of whom is not a member of your church.
- Look afresh at your personal and group finances. If you are able, decide to give some of your finances away to bless others in need. Who will you bless financially this week and in the weeks to come? Build generosity into your budget.
- Memorize Matthew 6:19-21, 24 and Matthew 6:2-4.

A SAMPLE PRAYER

Gracious God, fill our hearts with generosity.
Lead us away from greed and materialism,
and help us store up for ourselves treasures in heaven.
Help our hearts to be devoted to you alone;
let us never worship wealth or personal gains.
When we give, grant us the grace to give with humble hearts,
giving in secret to bless and enrich the lives of others.
You are a generous God.
Fill our hearts with a new commitment
to generosity, simplicity, and contentment.
Amen.

WEEK 3

Topic: Bless (Generosity)
Subtopic: Exhibit Practical Giving
Verses: 1 John 3:17-18 and 2 Corinthians 8:7

John says that we express genuine, Christ-imitating love through our actions and our practical giving. Jesus showed us the way when he laid down his life for us. When we see people in need we must give—this shows that the love of God is in us. "Let us not love with words or speech but with actions and in truth" (1 John 3:17-18).

Paul offers a stunning example of such generosity in 2 Corinthians 8. The Macedonian churches are suffering severe trials and extreme poverty, yet with overflowing joy and generosity they gave "as much as they were able, and even beyond their ability" (verse 3). They do this without being compelled, since they see generosity to others as a normal extension of giving themselves fully to the Lord. God calls us to excel in many areas of discipleship, including the "grace of giving" (2 Corinthians 8:7). Transformed disciples are generous disciples. Bless Christians and those who are not Christians through your giving.

YOUR PLAN THIS WEEK

- Use Monday to read 1 John 3:17-18 and 2 Corinthians 8:7 in their context. Reflect on their meaning in context and how to live them out in your life, church, and neighborhood. Notice that both passages are directed toward groups and their collective actions, not just individuals.

- Use Tuesday and Wednesday to memorize 1 John 3:17-18, and use Thursday and Friday to memorize 2 Corinthians 8:7. Use the weekend to practice the verses and to reflect on them.

- Take fifteen to twenty minutes each day to review the verses you've already learned. You may choose to write them down from memory. This will help ensure you don't forget them.

- Mark off the verses on the checklist once you've learned them.

- Work through the *Questions*, *Challenges*, and *Prayer* given below, alone or in a group. Modify them or add to them as you feel led by the Spirit.

QUESTIONS FOR MEDITATION AND GROUP REFLECTION

- Who will you bless this week? Name at least one person in your church and one person outside your church.
- Who has material need in your church and neighborhood? How are you loving them "with actions and in truth" (1 John 3:17-18)?
- What does it mean to "well up in rich generosity" (see 2 Corinthians 8:2), even in the midst of trials and poverty? How is generosity an expression of joy? How is God calling you to give as much as you are able, and even beyond your ability (2 Corinthians 8:7)?
- Why are generosity and practical giving an expression of giving yourself fully to the Lord (2 Corinthians 8:5)?
- How can we give to others to bless *them*, and not for our own benefit (see Philippians 2:3-4)?

CHALLENGES FOR YOU TO APPLY INDIVIDUALLY AND IN GROUPS

- Bless three people this week—at least one of whom is not a member of your church.
- Consider how your ideas for blessing others might be received, especially by people of different ethnic or socioeconomic backgrounds from you. Ask someone from a different background how you can bless them, and try to be completely open to their suggestions. What they ask you to do may surprise you, so be a humble learner and servant.
- Memorize 1 John 3:17-18 and 2 Corinthians 8:7.

A SAMPLE PRAYER

Lord, teach me to be generous,
to serve you as you deserve,
to give and not to count the cost,
to fight and not to heed the wounds,

to toil and not to seek for rest,
to labor and not to look for any reward,
save that of knowing that I do your holy will.
Amen.[2]

WEEK 4

Topic: Bless (Generosity)
Subtopic: Commit to Prayer
Verses: 1 Timothy 2:1-2 and Jeremiah 29:7

Praying for others is a way to bless them. Paul tells us to pray for all people, especially for leaders and rulers, that we may live peaceful and godly lives, and that all may come to saving faith and a knowledge of the truth (1 Timothy 2:1-4). As Christ's disciples, we follow his example in prayer. He prayed for God's Kingdom to come and God's will to be done, "on earth as it is in heaven" (Matthew 6:9-13). And he prayed for his disciples, the church, and the world (John 17).

We pray for the peace and prosperity of our neighbors and cities (Jeremiah 29:7) that all people may flourish, that God's people might prosper, and that all people would know the living God and the new life offered in Jesus Christ. Bless others by praying for them.

YOUR PLAN THIS WEEK

- Use Monday to read 1 Timothy 2:1-2 and Jeremiah 29:7 in their context. Reflect on their meaning in context and how to live them out in your life, church, and neighborhood. Notice that both these passages are directed toward groups and their collective actions, not just individuals.

- Use Tuesday and Wednesday to memorize 1 Timothy 2:1-2, and use Thursday and Friday to memorize Jeremiah 29:7. Use the weekend to practice the verses and to reflect on them.

- Take fifteen to twenty minutes each day to review the verses you've already learned. You may choose to write them down from memory. This will help ensure you don't forget them.

- Mark off the verses on the checklist once you've learned them.

- Work through the *Questions, Challenges,* and *Prayer* given below, alone or in a group. Modify them or add to them as you feel led by the Spirit.

- Ask someone to test you on all the verses you've learned so far. If you're learning together, then test each other. Make it an affirming and encouraging exercise.

QUESTIONS FOR MEDITATION AND GROUP REFLECTION

- Who will you bless this week? Name at least one person in your church and one person outside your church.
- Who are you praying for this week? Which neighborhood, community, and national leaders are you praying for? When you consider 1 Timothy 2:1-7, what do you think should be the content of your prayers?
- How are you praying for the peace and prosperity of your street, apartment block, neighborhood, city, and nation? What's the form and content of these prayers (Jeremiah 29:7)?

CHALLENGES FOR YOU TO APPLY INDIVIDUALLY AND IN GROUPS

- Bless three people this week—at least one of whom is not a member of your church.
- Spend twenty minutes each day praying for the people and leaders of your street, apartment block, neighborhood, city, and nation.
- Memorize 1 Timothy 2:1-2 and Jeremiah 29:7.

A SAMPLE PRAYER

Lord, you call us to pray without ceasing.

We pray for your mercy, freedom, healing, and strength
    for the broken and exploited,
    for the poor and the defenseless,
    for the sick and the dying,
    for the enslaved and oppressed.

We pray for our churches and world,
    for the peace and prosperity of our cities,
    for our neighbors and enemies,
    for those who rule and lead,
    for ministers and servants of your gospel,
    for those in traditions strange to us,
    for the races and religions represented in our neighborhoods.

We pray that you would move us beyond ourselves.

We pray for the courage to join with you as you move in the world,
    extending your Kingdom,
    bringing your justice and peace,
    healing antagonisms and conflicts,
    believing your signs and wonders,
    proclaiming your gospel and truth,
    loving unconditionally,
    being witnesses to faith, hope, and love,
    exalting your name in the world.

Make us a people of prayer.

We pray in the name of Jesus crucified and risen.
Amen.

Habit 2: Eat (Hospitality)

We eat together, sharing meals with believers and nonbelievers alike.

The second habit is eating with others. We'd like you to eat with three people each week—at least one of whom is a member of your church and at least one of whom is *not*. In *Surprise the World*, I (Michael) say that this habit is about hospitality. "The table ought to be the primary symbol of the Christian gathering. It represents hospitality, inclusivity, generosity, and grace. . . . The table is the great equalizer in relationships. When we eat together we discover the inherent humanity of all people."[3] As we welcome people outside the church to our tables, we often find they reciprocate, welcoming us to theirs.

Check the box next to each verse after you've memorized it:

Welcome Refugees and Immigrants
☐ Matthew 25:35-36, 40
☐ Deuteronomy 10:18-19

Show Hospitality and Welcome
☐ Luke 14:13-14
☐ Hebrews 13:2

Enjoy Table Fellowship
☐ Luke 7:34-35
☐ Luke 24:30-31

Show Justice, Mercy, Compassion
☐ Zechariah 7:9-10
☐ James 2:15-17

WEEK 5

Topic: Eat (Hospitality)
Subtopic: Welcome Refugees and Immigrants
Verses: Matthew 25:35-36, 40 and Deuteronomy 10:18-19

In Matthew 25, Jesus describes the moment when all the nations will be gathered before him and he will separate his true disciples from those who aren't his disciples (the sheep from the goats). What he says next is shocking. The mark of discipleship is feeding the hungry, giving water to the thirsty, welcoming the stranger, clothing those without clothes, and visiting and caring for the sick and imprisoned. "Whatever you did for one of the least of these brothers and sisters of mine, you did for me" (Matthew 25:40). Some have claimed that his use of "brothers and sisters" means that he's referring only to how we treat Christians, but that doesn't line up with Jesus' own actions. He means all those who are hungry, thirsty, strangers, naked, sick, and in prison (this list is only representative), since that's what he himself did.

Today, among the groups in most need of welcome and care are refugees, asylum seekers, and undocumented immigrants. The Lord God defends the cause of those who suffer need and injustice, and he loves the foreigner residing among you; he provides for their needs. "And you are to love those who are foreigners," remembering that you also were once foreigners and strangers (Deuteronomy 10:18-19). Hospitality isn't only about who we eat with; it's also about welcoming refugees and immigrants, as Christ himself welcomes them.

YOUR PLAN THIS WEEK

- Use Monday to read Matthew 25:35-36, 40 and Deuteronomy 10:18-19 in their context. Reflect on their meaning in context and how to live them out in your life, church, and neighborhood. Note that both of these passages are directed toward groups and their collective actions, not just individuals.

- Use Tuesday and Wednesday to memorize Matthew 25:35-36, 40, and use Thursday and Friday to memorize Deuteronomy 10:18-19. Use the weekend to practice the verses and to reflect on them.

- Take fifteen to twenty minutes each day to review the verses you've already learned. You may choose to write them down from memory. This will help ensure you don't forget them.

- Mark off the verses on the checklist once you've learned them.

- Work through the *Questions*, *Challenges*, and *Prayer* given below, alone or in a group. Modify them or add to them as you feel led by the Spirit.

QUESTIONS FOR MEDITATION AND GROUP REFLECTION

- Who will you eat with this week? Name at least one person in your church and one person outside your church.
- Reflect on the words of Matthew 25:35-36, 40. Who are the people in your community and neighborhood that you need to care for, feed, clothe, welcome, visit, and honor? Who are the "least of these" that Jesus calls his brothers and sisters and whom he expects you to love and serve?
- How do you feel about God loving and defending the fatherless, widowed, and foreigner among you? How will you respond to the call to "love those who are foreigners, for you yourselves were foreigners in Egypt" (Deuteronomy 10:18-19)?

CHALLENGES FOR YOU TO APPLY INDIVIDUALLY AND IN GROUPS

- Eat with three people this week—at least one of whom is not a member of your church. See if you can extend hospitality to an immigrant or refugee.
- Graham's website "The Global Church Project" (theglobalchurchproject.com) features resources on ministering

to and with immigrants and refugees. Go to the videos page, and search for Noel Castellanos or Lisa Rodriguez-Watson for videos and discussion questions about the needs of undocumented immigrants.

· Memorize Matthew 25:35-36, 40 and Deuteronomy 10:18-19.

A SAMPLE PRAYER

Lord, grant us compassion and courage to open our hearts, families,
lives, churches, and lands
to the foreigner and stranger,
to the homeless and stateless,
to those with no safe place to go,
to those with no passports or visas,
to the hungry and thirsty,
to the sick and imprisoned.

Whatever we do for the least of these, we do for you.
You are the one
who bends and breaks and demolishes
borders and boundaries and walls.

You call us to offer and to strive for
refuge for the asylum seeker,
safety for the persecuted,
shelter for the homeless,
welcome for the stranger and foreigner,
justice for the exploited,
healing for the wounded,
food for the hungry,
clothing for the naked,
freedom for the captive.

When we fret about refugees, asylum seekers, and immigrants, give us
your compassion for
preaching good news to the poor,
healing the brokenhearted,
liberating the captives,
releasing the imprisoned,
welcoming the rejected,
sheltering the endangered,
demolishing walls and divisions,
comforting those who mourn,
proclaiming, in word and sign and deed,
the year of the Lord's favor.

We pray in the name of your holy Son, our Lord Jesus.
Amen.

WEEK 6

Topic: Eat (Hospitality)
Subtopic: Show Hospitality and Welcome
Verses: Luke 14:13-14 and Hebrews 13:2

Often when we organize a dinner or lunch, we invite friends, family, and respectable neighbors. Then they invite us back, so there's a personal and social payoff. But Jesus says that we should show hospitality and welcome to the poor, the crippled, the lame, the blind, the unlovely, the undesirable, and those who often can't repay our welcome and generosity. Such welcome imitates the love and embrace of God in Jesus Christ, and God repays at the resurrection of the righteous (Luke 14:13-14). Jesus also calls us to show hospitality to foreigners, neighbors, and strangers (Hebrews 13:2; Deuteronomy 10:18-19; and other verses). Such hospitality and welcome imitates Christ, blesses others, reveals the gospel, and glorifies God.

- Use Monday to read Luke 14:13-14 and Hebrews 13:2 in their context. Reflect on their meaning in context and how to live them out in your life, church, and neighborhood. Notice that both of these passages are directed toward groups and their collective actions, not just individuals.

- Use Tuesday and Wednesday to memorize Luke 14:13-14, and use Thursday and Friday to memorize Hebrews 13:2. Use the weekend to practice the verses and to reflect on them.

- Take fifteen to twenty minutes each day to review the verses you've already learned. You may choose to write them down from memory. This will help ensure you don't forget them.

- Mark off the verses on the checklist once you've learned them.

- Work through the *Questions, Challenges,* and *Prayer* given below, alone or in a group. Modify them or add to them as you feel led by the Spirit.

QUESTIONS FOR MEDITATION AND GROUP REFLECTION

- Who will you eat with this week? Name at least one person in your church and one person outside your church.
- Read Luke 14:7-14. How is the Spirit calling you to live in light of this passage, specifically the words, "For all those who exalt themselves will be humbled, and those who humble themselves will be exalted" (verse 11)?
- Who are the modern-day "poor, . . . crippled, . . . lame, . . . blind" that you are inviting to your table? When are they eating at your table (Luke 14:13-14)?
- Are you showing hospitality to strangers (Hebrews 13:2)? If so, how? What forms of hospitality and welcome can we show strangers?

CHALLENGES FOR YOU TO APPLY INDIVIDUALLY AND IN GROUPS

- Eat with three people this week—at least one of whom is not a member of your church.
- Pray with a friend, partner, spouse, or small group for opportunities to show welcome and hospitality to strangers. Then look for those opportunities and take them.
- Memorize Luke 14:13-14 and Hebrews 13:2.

A SAMPLE PRAYER

Release us from the desire to be esteemed and noticed,
free us from the drive to be praised and honored,
and lead us into your humility.
Open our hearts to those who are not honored by the world;
and make our tables places of welcome and hospitality.
Cause us to see your presence and hear your voice
among the poor, broken, rejected, and forgotten,
so that we would welcome and honor them the way you do.
Help us open our homes, our families, our lands, and our lives
to the foreigner and stranger,
just as you welcomed and loved us.
Amen.

WEEK 7

Topic: Eat (Hospitality)
Subtopic: Enjoy Table Fellowship
Verses: Luke 7:34-35 and Luke 24:30-31

We often think of the Son of Man coming to serve, to give his life as a ransom for many, and to seek and save the lost (Mark 10:45; Luke 19:10). But the Son of Man also came "eating and drinking"

(Luke 7:34-35). He was accused of being a drunk and glutton who enjoyed table fellowship with sinners, tax collectors, prostitutes, and the least desirable people in society. He also told his disciples to eat together every time they met. Table fellowship was at the heart of Jesus' ministry and mission, and it's also at the heart of the church's mission and ministry today. We change the world by eating: eating together and eating with the poor, the political and ethnic "other," the stranger, and the neighbor. After traveling with Jesus on the road to Emmaus, the two disciples recognized Jesus when he ate with them because table fellowship was so central to his life with them (Luke 24:30-31). We see Jesus—and truly see others in all their value and humanity—around tables.

YOUR PLAN THIS WEEK

- Use Monday to read Luke 7:34-35 and Luke 24:30-31 in their context. Reflect on their meaning in context and how to live them out in your life, church, and neighborhood. Notice that both of these passages are directed toward groups and their collective actions, not just individuals.

- Use Tuesday and Wednesday to memorize Luke 7:34-35, and use Thursday and Friday to memorize Luke 24:30-31. Use the weekend to practice the verses and to reflect on them.

- Take fifteen to twenty minutes each day to review the verses you've already learned. You may choose to write them down from memory. This will help ensure you don't forget them.

- Mark off the verses on the checklist once you've learned the verses.

- Work through the *Questions*, *Challenges*, and *Prayer* given below, alone or in a group. Modify them or add to them as you feel led by the Spirit.

QUESTIONS FOR MEDITATION AND GROUP REFLECTION

- Who will you eat with this week? Name at least one person in your church and one person outside your church.
- Who are you eating with that might cause a scandal, or at least be surprising for religious types (Luke 7:34-35)?
- Why do you think the Emmaus disciples only recognized Jesus when he ate with them? And what resonances are there between Luke 24:30-31 and the Lord's Supper? Is this significant?
- On what other occasions in Jesus' life did he eat with people, and why was this table fellowship significant? Why did Jesus place so much emphasis on eating with people?
- How did the early church follow Jesus' practice of eating with unlikely people? How will you?

CHALLENGES FOR YOU TO APPLY INDIVIDUALLY AND IN GROUPS

- Eat with three people this week—at least one of whom is not a member of your church. Share a meal with someone this week whom you wouldn't normally eat with (preferably someone from your workplace or neighborhood).
- Memorize Luke 7:34-35 and Luke 24:30-31.

A SAMPLE PRAYER

Lord Jesus, we know that whom we welcome or exclude from our table shows the condition of our hearts. You came eating and drinking. Give us the grace to do the same. Let our tables be places of welcome and hospitality for believers, strangers, foreigners, and enemies. Grant that meals around our tables would be gatherings of hospitality, inclusivity, generosity, and grace. Let our tables be places of love and laughter, tears and grieving, prayer and conversation, honesty and vulnerability, messiness and human touch. Jesus, join us at our tables as the host who is always welcoming us to your table. Amen.

WEEK 8

Topic: Eat (Hospitality)
Subtopic: Show Justice, Mercy, Compassion
Verses: Zechariah 7:9-10 and James 2:15-17

God loves justice, mercy, and compassion because these are his own qualities. There is no mercy without justice, no justice without compassion, and no compassion without mercy. All three need the others to reveal Christ and his gospel. And God's welcome and hospitality flow from the fact that he is a just, merciful, and compassionate God. We imitate Christ when our welcome of others overflows in practical acts of advocacy, solidarity, justice, care, and compassion. "Administer true justice; show mercy and compassion to one another. Do not oppress the widow or the fatherless, the foreigner or the poor" (Zechariah 7:9-10). Our faith is manifest and proven in our actions (James 2:15-17). Our faith and discipleship are shown and verified through our just deeds, merciful actions, compassionate behaviors, and hospitable hearts.

YOUR PLAN THIS WEEK

- Use Monday to read Zechariah 7:9-10 and James 2:15-17 in their context. Reflect on their meaning in context and how to live them out in your life, church, and neighborhood. Notice that both these passages are directed toward groups and their collective actions, not just individuals.

- Use Tuesday and Wednesday to memorize Zechariah 7:9-10, and use Thursday and Friday to memorize James 2:15-17. Use the weekend to practice the verses and to reflect on them.

- Take fifteen to twenty minutes each day to review the verses you've already learned. You may choose to write them down from memory. This will help ensure you don't forget them.

- Mark off the verses on the checklist once you've learned them.

- Work through the *Questions*, *Challenges*, and *Prayer* given below, alone or in a group. Modify them or add to them as you feel led by the Spirit.

QUESTIONS FOR MEDITATION AND GROUP REFLECTION

- Who will you eat with this week? Name at least one person in your church and one person outside your church.
- What are some practical ways that you and your church or small group can "administer true justice" and "show mercy and compassion" (Zechariah 7:9)?
- How is God calling you to respond compassionately to the physical needs of people in your neighborhood? How will you respond to the physical needs of other groups in your nation or overseas (James 2:15-17)?

CHALLENGES FOR YOU TO APPLY INDIVIDUALLY AND IN GROUPS

- Eat with three people this week—at least one of whom is not a member of your church.
- Do one act of compassion this week. There are many compassionate things you can do! Here are some examples: Help an elderly neighbor do their gardening or paint their house. Organize meals for a person or family in need. Visit people in the hospital or in a nursing home. Serve in a soup kitchen.
- Memorize Zechariah 7:9-10 and James 2:15-17.

A SAMPLE PRAYER

*You move us with your compassion
and fill us with your love.*

You make our love sincere
and our actions full of your mercy.

You lead us to rejoice with those who rejoice
and weep with those who weep.

You cause our lives to reflect your compassion,
administer your true justice,
show your mercy and compassion,
proclaim your Good News to the poor,
freedom for the captives,
recovery of sight for the blind,
and the year of the Lord's favor.

You make our prayers passionate,
our lives just,
our words loving,
our actions merciful,
our hearts compassionate.

Amen.

Habit 3: Listen (Spirit-led)

We listen to the guidance and direction of the
Holy Spirit as we engage with those around us.

The third habit is listening for the Spirit's voice. We'd like you to spend at least one period of the week listening for the Spirit's voice. In *Surprise the World*, I (Michael) say that

> as we become more familiar with listening to the Spirit as a
> kind of weekly rhythm, we'll also find ourselves becoming
> more adept at hearing the Spirit in real time, in the midst of

encounters with our neighbors, as we bless or share a meal
or otherwise get in the way of the people around us. That's
why listening to the Spirit is one of the five habits of highly
missional people.[4]

In *Healing Our Broken Humanity*, I (Graham) say the Spirit empowers the church for mission. The Spirit works through us to "bring
liberation, healing, justice, mercy, and hope to a broken world. In
doing so the Spirit empowers the church to witness to divine love and
reconciliation."[5]

Check the box next to each verse after you've memorized it:

Repent and Lament
☐ Acts 3:19-20
☐ Joel 2:12-13

Be Peacemakers
☐ Matthew 5:9
☐ Romans 12:14, 18

Seek Guidance and Direction
☐ Psalm 25:4-5
☐ Proverbs 2:6-9

Be Disciplined and Corrected
☐ Hebrews 12:7-8, 11
☐ Revelation 3:19

WEEK 9

Topic: Listen (Spirit-Led)
Subtopic: Repent and Lament
Verses: Acts 3:19-20 and Joel 2:12-13

Our lives can be so busy and frenetic that we can fail to stop and hear the Spirit calling us to discipleship. But we need quiet hearts to hear the Spirit and his call to repentance and renewal. The words of Scripture and the voice of the Spirit call us to repent of our pride, greed, lust, envy, self-indulgence, anger, violence, racism, sexism, fear, antagonism, and laziness. They lament the way our fear and laziness have killed our mission and witness. But there is hope and new life in repentance! "Repent, then, and turn to God, so that your sins may be wiped out, that times of refreshing may come from the Lord, and that he may send the Messiah, who has been appointed for you—even Jesus" (Acts 3:19-20). If we listen to the Spirit, we'll hear him calling us to rend our hearts, lament our sin, and return to God "with fasting and weeping and mourning" (Joel 2:12-13). New life comes from our gracious, compassionate, and loving God as we return to him in lament and repentance.

YOUR PLAN THIS WEEK

- Use Monday to read Acts 3:19-20 and Joel 2:12-13 in their context. Reflect on their meaning in context and how to live them out in your life, church, and neighborhood. Notice that both these passages are directed toward groups and their collective actions, not just individuals.

- Use Tuesday and Wednesday to memorize Acts 3:19-20, and use Thursday and Friday to memorize Joel 2:12-13. Use the weekend to practice the verses and to reflect on them.

- Take fifteen to twenty minutes each day to review the verses you've already learned. You may choose to write them down from memory. This will help ensure you don't forget them.

- Mark off the verses on the checklist once you've learned the verses.

- Work through the *Questions*, *Challenges*, and *Prayer* given below, alone or in a group. Modify them or add to them as you feel led by the Spirit.

QUESTIONS FOR MEDITATION AND GROUP REFLECTION

- How are you learning to listen to the Spirit's voice in your daily life?
- Why do we sometimes find it difficult to sit with the discomfort of lament?
- We know Jesus has died for our sins and that there is no condemnation for us in him. But why is there still value in lamenting over our failings and those of others?
- What kinds of things do people in your culture typically need to repent of? Why does the church need to repent of these things too?

CHALLENGES FOR YOU TO APPLY INDIVIDUALLY AND IN GROUPS

- Spend at least one period of this week listening for the Spirit's voice.
- Don't avoid the discomfort of lament. Allow yourself to be present to that deep, genuine sadness about the brokenness in the world and in you.
- Confess your sins, both the choices you've made that dishonor Christ and the decisions you've avoided that you know Christ wants you to make.
- Memorize Acts 3:19-20 and Joel 2:12-13.

A SAMPLE PRAYER:

Father, grant us the grace to lament and repent
for those times when we have
worshiped money and status,
pursued power and control,
confused religious patriotism with Christian discipleship,
sanctioned violence,
ignored or excused abuse and exploitation,
embraced individualism,

fostered disunity and conflict,
fueled antagonism,
excused family violence and child abuse,
cultivated racism and sexism,
closed our hearts to refugees and immigrants,
focused on image and brand,
shunned those who are different from us,
indulged in pornography,
abused the earth and the poor,
encouraged exceptionalism and nationalism,
excluded the unlovely and undesirable.

Have mercy on us, O God,
according to your unfailing love;
according to your great compassion,
blot out our transgressions.
Wash away all our iniquities,
and cleanse us from our sin.

Create in us a pure heart, O God,
and renew a steadfast, repentant, holy spirit within us.
Our sacrifice, O God, is a broken spirit;
a broken and contrite heart, O God, you will not despise.
Open our lips, O Lord, and our mouths will declare your
praise.
Open our hearts and lives, that we may be like you.
Amen.[6]

WEEK 10

Topic: Listen (Spirit-Led)
Subtopic: Be Peacemakers
Verses: Matthew 5:9 and Romans 12:14, 18

Jesus said, "Blessed are the peacemakers, for they will be called children of God" (Matthew 5:9). The Spirit of Jesus is always leading us toward peacemaking and reconciliation. We sometimes misunderstand peacemaking. Shane Claiborne, Jonathan Wilson-Hartgrove, and Enuma Okoro say:

> Peacemaking doesn't mean passivity. It is the act of interrupting injustice without mirroring injustice, the act of disarming evil without destroying the evildoer, the act of finding a third way that is neither fight nor flight but the careful, arduous pursuit of reconciliation and justice. It is about a revolution of love that is big enough to set both the oppressed and the oppressors free. . . .
>
> Peacemaking . . . "'that is not like any way the empire brings peace' is rooted in the nonviolence of the cross, where we see a Savior who loves his enemies so much he died for them."[7]

We live in an age of conflict and antagonism. Rage is everywhere. But instead of fueling anger, violence, and division, we follow the Spirit of Christ, who leads us into peace and to be peacemakers. "Bless those who persecute you; bless and do not curse. . . . If it is possible, as far as it depends on you, live at peace with everyone" (Romans 12:14, 18). We are called God's children when we follow the Spirit's leading into peacemaking.

YOUR PLAN THIS WEEK

- Use Monday to read Matthew 5:9 and Romans 12:14, 18 in their context. Reflect on their meaning in context, and how to live them out in your life, church, and neighborhood. Notice that both these passages are directed toward groups and their collective actions, not just individuals.

- Use Tuesday and Wednesday to memorize Matthew 5:9, and use Thursday and Friday to memorize Romans 12:14, 18. Use the weekend to practice the verses and to reflect on them.

- Take fifteen to twenty minutes each day to review the verses you've already learned. You may choose to write them down from memory. This will help ensure you don't forget them.

- Mark off the verses on the checklist once you've learned them.

- Work through the *Questions*, *Challenges*, and *Prayer* given below, alone or in a group. Modify them or add to them as you feel led by the Spirit.

QUESTIONS FOR MEDITATION AND GROUP REFLECTION

- When will you spend at least one period of this week listening for the Spirit's voice?
- How does the Spirit cultivate peace of mind in your life?
- What is the relationship between having "inner" peace and being a peacemaker in a troubled world?
- What does it mean for you to live at peace with everyone (a) in your neighborhood, (b) in your church, (c) on social media?
- What peacemaking initiatives are you associated with or committed to? If none, ask the Spirit to prompt you about how to become a peacemaker.

CHALLENGES FOR YOU TO APPLY INDIVIDUALLY AND IN GROUPS

- Spend at least one period of this week listening for the Spirit's voice.
- If you're not involved in any peacemaking initiatives, take some time to research groups, organizations, and online forums that you might consider becoming involved with.
- Memorize Matthew 5:9 and Romans 12:14, 18.

Lord Jesus, lead us, together, to your cross.
  The cross is the way of peacemakers.
  The cross is the support for those who stumble.
  The cross is the guide for the blind.
  The cross is the strength of the weak.
  The cross is the hope of the hopeless.
  The cross is the freedom of the enslaved.
  The cross is the water of the seeds.
  The cross is the consolation of the suffering.
  The cross is the voice of the voiceless.
  The cross is the source of those who seek water.
  The cross is the cloth of the naked.
  The cross is the faith of the doubter.
  The cross is the offer of welcome and embrace for those excluded.
  The cross is the holy rage against injustice.
  The cross is the healing of the broken.
  The cross is the justice of the wronged.
  The cross is the reconciliation of those in conflict.
  The cross is the cure to violence and vengeance.
  The cross is the fellowship of his sufferings.
  The cross is the comfort for those who lament and mourn.
  The cross is the hope of a new creation and a new humanity.
  The cross is the love for those who are enemies.
  The cross is the way of peace and reconciliation.
  The cross is the peace of the world and the church.
  Lord Jesus, lead us, together, to your cross.[8]

WEEK 11

Topic: Listen (Spirit-Led)
Subtopic: Seek Guidance and Direction
Verses: Psalm 25:4-5 and Proverbs 2:6-9

We need to create space for solitude, silence, and prayer if we are to hear and follow the Spirit's voice. The Psalms can help shape our prayers during those times. People have prayed the Psalms individually and together for many generations. People in solitude and congregations together have prayed "show me [us] your ways, teach me [us] your paths. Guide me [us] in your truth and teach me, for . . . my [our] hope is in you" (see Psalm 25:4-5). When we pray such prayers, the missional voice of the Spirit prompts us to adjust our attitudes, strengthen our resolve, overcome our fears, and join with God in mission and service. The Spirit of Christ gives us wisdom, knowledge, and understanding and shows us "what is right and just and fair—every good path" (Proverbs 2:6-9).

YOUR PLAN THIS WEEK

- Use Monday to read Psalm 25:4-5 and Proverbs 2:6-9 in their context. Reflect on their meaning in context and how to live them out in your life, church, and neighborhood. Notice that both these passages are directed toward groups and their collective actions, not just individuals.

- Use Tuesday and Wednesday to memorize Psalm 25:4-5, and use Thursday and Friday to memorize Proverbs 2:6-9. Use the weekend to practice the verses and to reflect on them.

- Take fifteen to twenty minutes each day to review the verses you've already learned. You may choose to write them down from memory. This will help ensure you don't forget them.

- Mark off the verses on the checklist once you've learned them.

- Work through the *Questions*, *Challenges*, and *Prayer* given below, alone or in a group. Modify them or add to them as you feel led by the Spirit.

QUESTIONS FOR MEDITATION AND GROUP REFLECTION

- When will you spend at least one period of this week listening for the Spirit's voice?
- In what areas of your life are you seeking the Lord's guidance?
- How will you commit yourself to seeking the Spirit's guidance for the path that you must walk?
- Specifically, what gets in the way of you hearing from God?
- What routines or practices do you need to adopt to allow the time to hear the Spirit's guidance?

CHALLENGES FOR YOU TO APPLY INDIVIDUALLY AND IN GROUPS

- Spend at least one period of this week listening for the Spirit's voice.
- Read chapter 5 of *Surprise the World*. In that chapter, there are several ideas for how to hear the Spirit's voice.
- Seriously consider whether any of the areas you're seeking guidance in relate to justice, peacemaking, and reconciliation, rather than solely personal issues.
- Memorize Psalm 25:4-5 and Proverbs 2:6-9.

A SAMPLE PRAYER

Heavenly Father,
  show us your ways,
  teach us your paths,
  guide us in your truth,
  teach us your justice, mercy, and humility,
  lead us to imitate and conform to your Son.

For you are our God and Savior,
  and our hope is in you all day long.

May your Spirit guide and direct us;
your ways are perfect, and your grace is sufficient.

Amen.

WEEK 12

Topic: Listen (Spirit-Led)
Subtopic: Be Disciplined and Corrected
Verses: Hebrews 12:7-8, 11 and Revelation 3:19

Sometimes the Spirit needs to discipline and correct us, individually and together, so that we can continue conforming to the love, holiness, and image of Christ. God disciplines us because he loves us and accepts us as his children. This discipline can be unpleasant and even painful. "Later on, however, it produces a harvest of righteousness and peace for those who have been trained by it" (Hebrews 12:11). God loves those he rebukes and disciplines, and our appropriate response is to be earnest and repentant (Revelation 3:19). Being led by the Spirit can be uncomfortable and even painful—but God is conforming us into the image of the Son he loves.

YOUR PLAN THIS WEEK

- Use Monday to read Hebrews 12:7-8, 11 and Revelation 3:19 in their context. Reflect on their meaning in context and how to live them out in your life, church, and neighborhood. Notice that both these passages are directed toward groups and their collective actions, not just individuals.

- Use Tuesday and Wednesday to memorize Hebrews 12:7-8, 11, and use Thursday and Friday to memorize Revelation 3:19. Use the weekend to practice the verses and to reflect on them.

- Take fifteen to twenty minutes each day to review the verses you've already learned. You may choose to write them down from memory. This will help ensure you don't forget them.

- Mark off the verses on the checklist once you've learned them.

- Work through the *Questions, Challenges,* and *Prayer* given below, alone or in a group. Modify them or add to them as you feel led by the Spirit.

QUESTIONS FOR MEDITATION AND GROUP REFLECTION

- When will you spend at least one period of this week listening for the Spirit's voice?
- How do you personally experience the discipline/correction of God?
- Can you say, as in Proverbs 12:1, that you love discipline? If not, why not?
- Why do you think the writer of Hebrews commends discipline and correction as strongly as he does?
- What stops you from seeing God's discipline in your life as an act of love?

CHALLENGES FOR YOU TO APPLY INDIVIDUALLY AND IN GROUPS

- Spend at least one period of this week listening for the Spirit's voice.
- In most Christian traditions, repentance is demonstrated by (a) godly sorrow, (b) confession of sin, and (c) appropriate deeds, or restitution. How are you seeking to confess your sins to an accountability group or mentor?
- Discussion around issues of reconciliation is richer in diverse groups. Make special effort to include members of marginalized or minority communities—people who are poor or people from

ethnic minority communities—in conversations and reflections about race relations and systemic injustice where you live. Then ask, "How is the Spirit disciplining our group and calling us to respond and change?"

- Memorize Hebrews 12:7-8, 11 and Revelation 3:19.

A SAMPLE PRAYER

Father, discipline and correct us in your love. Give us the strength to reject drunkenness, gossip, and gluttony, and refuse judgmentalism, pharisaism, and pietism. Set our minds on Christ and our hearts on what the Spirit desires. Let our lives glorify you. May the Spirit move in our lives, that we might grieve and repent of sin, crave your presence, grow in your Spirit, and bear witness to the gospel of your Son. Rebuke and discipline us in your love; grant us the grace to be earnest and repentant. In Jesus' name, Amen.

Habit 4: Learn (Christlike)

We intimately learn Christ as our leader and model for making disciples.

The fourth habit is learning Christ. We'd like you to spend at least one period of the week learning Christ. This habit is about growing in Christlikeness. In *Surprise the World*, I (Michael) say,

I think that if we're being sent into the world to live intriguing lives, arouse curiosity, and answer people's inquiries about the hope we have within, we need more than ever to know what Jesus would do or say in any circumstance. And we can't know that without a deep and ongoing study of the biographies of Jesus written by those who knew him best—the Gospels. . . .

The church needs to be immersed again in the Gospels, totally marinated in the work and words of Jesus.[9]

Check the box next to each verse after you've memorized it:

Love God, Neighbors, and Enemies
☐ Mark 12:30-31
☐ Matthew 5:43-46

Seek Reconciliation
☐ 2 Corinthians 5:18
☐ Colossians 1:19-20

Display Humility and Self-Sacrifice
☐ Philippians 2:3-4
☐ Matthew 16:24-25

Proclaim Freedom and Gospel
☐ Luke 4:18-19
☐ Romans 1:16-17

WEEK 13

Topic: Learn (Christlike)
Subtopic: Love God, Neighbors, and Enemies
Verses: Mark 12:30-31 and Matthew 5:43-46

Jesus was asked by a religious leader, "Of all the commandments, which is the most important?" His answer was clear. "Love the Lord your God with all your heart and with all your soul and with all your mind and with all your strength. . . . Love your neighbor as yourself" (Mark 12:28-31). Being Christlike means loving God and loving your neighbor. Loving your neighbors means welcoming them to your table and practicing justice, mercy, care, and compassion toward your fellow human beings.

Mark 12:32-34 says that loving God and loving your neighbor as yourself are more important than all other religious rituals and observances, since such love is Christlike and a witness to his Kingdom. But Jesus takes it even further. Jesus says that we are not only to love our neighbor but also to love our enemies, praying for those who persecute and attack us (Matthew 5:43-46). Such love of God, neighbor, and enemy is world-changing—it reflects the love of God, heals wounds and divisions, breaks down walls and barriers, joins with God in his mission, witnesses to the gospel of Christ, and imitates the sacrifice and divine love of Jesus.

YOUR PLAN THIS WEEK

- Use Monday to read Mark 12:30-31 and Matthew 5:43-46 in their context. Reflect on their meaning in context and how to live them out in your life, church, and neighborhood. Notice that both these passages are directed toward groups and their collective actions, not just individuals.

- Use Tuesday and Wednesday to memorize Mark 12:30-31, and use Thursday and Friday to memorize Matthew 5:43-46. Use the weekend to practice the verses and to reflect on them.

- Take fifteen to twenty minutes each day to review the verses you've already learned. You may choose to write them down from memory. This will help ensure you don't forget them.

- Mark off the verses on the checklist once you've learned them.

- Work through the *Questions*, *Challenges*, and *Prayer* given below, alone or in a group. Modify them or add to them as you feel led by the Spirit.

QUESTIONS FOR MEDITATION AND GROUP REFLECTION

- During this week, how will you spend at least one period of the week learning Christ?
- In a recent tweet, Brian Zahnd said, "The biblical test case for love of God is love of neighbor. The biblical test case for love of

neighbor is love of enemy."[10] How do you feel about this quote? How does it reflect the words of Jesus in Mark 12:30-31 and Matthew 5:43-46?

- Why is there no greater commandment than to love God and to love your neighbor (Mark 12:30-31)?
- Who are your enemies? How are you praying for them and for those who persecute you? What are practical ways we can show our enemies and/or opponents that we love them (Matthew 5:43-46)?

CHALLENGES FOR YOU TO APPLY INDIVIDUALLY AND IN GROUPS

- Spend at least one period of the week learning Christ.
- Write a list of all those who are your enemies (or with whom you are in conflict). Do the following this week (or during this month): Pray for God's help to forgive them. Pray for them. Consider and empathize with their point of view. Do some self-reflection on where the animosity and your feelings come from. Let go of resentments and anger, with God's help, through prayer (sometimes this requires counseling). Speak well of them. Do good to them when you have an opportunity. Recognize that loving enemies is hard, that it can't be done without God's help, and that it's a lifetime commitment.
- Memorize Mark 12:30-31 and Matthew 5:43-46.

A SAMPLE PRAYER

Lord Jesus, help us love God with all our heart and soul and mind and strength. Help us love our neighbor as ourselves. We let go of unforgiveness, envy, animosity, prejudice, racism, and pride. Enable us to show your embrace and love and welcome. Move us to include and embrace those who are different from us: those of a different faith, ethnicity, gender, political persuasion, race, and more. May your Spirit enable us to love our enemies and pray for those who persecute us, that we truly live as children of our Father in heaven. You call us to love and bless and pray for our enemies; give us the strength and wisdom to do just that. Amen.

WEEK 14

Topic: Learn (Christlike)
Subtopic: Seek Reconciliation
Verses: 2 Corinthians 5:18 and Colossians 1:19-20

Jesus is the great reconciler, who reconciles us to God and gives us the ministry of reconciliation (2 Corinthians 5:18). God is the source of reconciliation. Christ is the revelation of reconciliation. We are the ambassadors of reconciliation. We join with God as he reconciles people to himself, to themselves, to each other, and to creation. To be reconcilers is to be Christlike.

Jesus Christ is "the image of the invisible God, the firstborn over all creation," the creator and sustainer of all things, the fullness of God, the head of the church, and the agent of God's reconciliation. Through Jesus, all things in heaven and earth are reconciled to God, since Jesus made peace through his blood, shed on the cross (Colossians 1:15-23). Jesus reconciles people with God, and he also enables reconciliation between the nations, races, sexes, classes, and peoples of the world. Be Christlike; be a reconciler.

YOUR PLAN THIS WEEK

- Use Monday to read 2 Corinthians 5:18 and Colossians 1:19-20 in their context. Reflect on their meaning in context and how to live them out in your life, church, and neighborhood. Notice that both these passages are directed toward groups and their collective actions, not just individuals.

- Use Tuesday and Wednesday to memorize 2 Corinthians 5:18, and use Thursday and Friday to memorize Colossians 1:19-20. Use the weekend to practice the verses and to reflect on them.

- Take fifteen to twenty minutes each day to review the verses you've already learned. You may choose to write them down from memory. This will help ensure you don't forget them.

- Mark off the verses on the checklist once you've learned them.

- Work through the *Questions, Challenges,* and *Prayer* given below, alone or in a group. Modify them or add to them as you feel led by the Spirit.

QUESTIONS FOR MEDITATION AND GROUP REFLECTION

- During this week, how will you spend at least one period of the week learning Christ?
- In *Roadmap to Reconciliation,* Brenda Salter McNeil defines *reconciliation* in a helpful way. Her definition talks about the biblical and theological *foundations* of reconciliation, the various *aspects* of reconciliation, the *process* of reconciliation, the *systemic nature* of reconciliation, and the *final goal* of reconciliation. McNeil says, "Reconciliation is an ongoing spiritual process involving forgiveness, repentance and justice that restores broken relationships and systems to reflect God's original intention for all creation to flourish."[11] How would you modify this definition? Or how would you put it in your own words?
- Read through 2 Corinthians 5:11–6:2. What are some practical ways God is calling your family, small group, or church to the ministry of reconciliation?
- What are some practical things you can do to ensure that your church's reconciling actions and ministries glorify Jesus Christ and reflect his passion for reconciliation? (See Colossians 1:15-23.)

CHALLENGES FOR YOU TO APPLY INDIVIDUALLY AND IN GROUPS

- Spend at least one period of the week learning Christ.
- Watch some movies and documentaries alone or, even better, in a small group or ministry team. Natasha Sistrunk Robinson has put together a list of movies and documentaries that stimulate discussion about race, justice, and reconciliation.[12] Develop your own list. Here are the movies that we have found most insightful, provocative, and discussion generating: *12 Years a Slave, District 9, Hotel Rwanda, Schindler's List, Belle, The Visitor.* In your small group, get together regularly for meals and to watch these and other relevant movies. Discuss what you learn from them about race, racism, justice, and reconciliation. Note that discussions about race and systemic injustice are much richer when the people participating represent a broad spectrum, so consider how you might include in your discussions people of different ethnic or socioeconomic backgrounds.
- Memorize 2 Corinthians 5:18 and Colossians 1:19-20.

A SAMPLE PRAYER

Before you our Creator, Redeemer and Sustainer
We remember that we stand on holy ground

We acknowledge the stories of this land
We acknowledge the peoples of this land
We acknowledge the lore of this land
We acknowledge the languages of this land

We acknowledge that this land and her peoples
are in need of healing

Give us compassion

to hear and to feel the pain of lives torn apart
to hear and feel the pain of land that is damaged and mistreated
—sold to the highest bidder

Give us conviction
to name where we benefit from the dispossession of First Peoples
to see where injustice has taken hold
and to not look away

Give us courage
to listen; to see; to feel; to name
the pain,
the loss,
the theft and
the resistance

May we be inspired by truth-tellers,
justice-seekers and peacemakers in every age

Turn our inaction into action

We pray this in the name of Jesus the Christ,
Amen.[13]

WEEK 15

Topic: Learn (Christlike)
Subtopic: Display Humility and Self-Sacrifice
Verses: Philippians 2:3-4 and Matthew 16:24-25

Humility wasn't prized in the Greco-Roman culture. Jesus brought a humility revolution into the world. John Dickson says that Jesus talked about humility and service and self-sacrifice, but it was his execution on a cross that established the Christian idea of humility. Jesus' crucifixion upended notions of greatness, teaching us that greatness is expressed in humility, in choosing to lower oneself for the sake of others, and "in a willingness to hold power in service of others."[14]

Paul instructs the Philippian church to imitate Christ's humility and self-sacrifice. "Do nothing out of selfish ambition or vain conceit. Rather, in humility value others above yourselves, not looking to your own interests but each of you to the interests of others" (Philippians 2:3-4). Paul then moves into a marvelous Christological hymn, celebrating the humility, sacrifice, and glory of Christ. Denying ourselves, taking up our cross, and following Jesus—these things imitate Christ, glorify God, and lead us to fullness of life (Matthew 16:24-25).

YOUR PLAN THIS WEEK

- Use Monday to read Philippians 2:3-4 and Matthew 16:24-25 in their context. Reflect on their meaning in context and how to live them out in your life, church, and neighborhood. Notice that both these passages are directed toward groups and their collective actions, not just individuals.

- Use Tuesday and Wednesday to memorize Philippians 2:3-4, and use Thursday and Friday to memorize Matthew 16:24-25. Use the weekend to practice the verses and to reflect on them.

- Take fifteen to twenty minutes each day to review the verses you've already learned. You may choose to write them down from memory. This will help ensure you don't forget them.

- Mark off the verses on the checklist once you've learned them.

- Work through the *Questions, Challenges,* and *Prayer* given below, alone or in a group. Modify them or add to them as you feel led by the Spirit.

QUESTIONS FOR MEDITATION AND GROUP REFLECTION

- During this week, how will you spend at least one period of the week learning Christ?
- In the first part of Philippians 2, Paul talks about unity and humility. Why is humility a radical and subversive posture in today's world?
- What are practical, everyday ways we can live out the teachings to "value others above yourselves, not looking to your own interests but each of you to the interests of others" (Philippians 2:3-4)?
- Read Matthew 16:24-28. What are the costs and sacrifices associated with discipleship and following Jesus?
- Jesus says, "Whoever loses their life for me will find it." What experience do you have of this? (See Matthew 16:24-25.)

CHALLENGES FOR YOU TO APPLY INDIVIDUALLY AND IN GROUPS

- Spend at least one period of the week learning Christ.
- Spend this week acknowledging other people's achievements and giving them credit. Say nothing about yourself all week. Acknowledge and honor other people's achievements in your conversations, in group meetings, and on social media.
- We sometimes think that self-sacrifice must be shown in large and dramatic ways (like the accomplishments of Mother Teresa or Florence Nightingale). Sometimes it is a large sacrifice, as when someone follows God's call to give up a lucrative career to serve God in mission. But most self-sacrifice happens in small, daily, self-sacrificial acts. Sacrificial living happens when we offer our time, money, possessions, ambitions, rights, words, sexuality, dreams, and will to God. Eugene Peterson puts it this way, "So here's what I want you to do, God helping you: Take your

everyday, ordinary life—your sleeping, eating, going-to-work, and walking-around life—and place it before God as an offering" (Romans 12:1-2, MSG). It's in these daily acts that we often "deny [ourselves] and take up [our] cross and follow [Jesus]" (Matthew 16:24). Write a list of ways you are going to do this over the following weeks, and then put them into action.

• Memorize Philippians 2:3-4 and Matthew 16:24-25.

A SAMPLE PRAYER:

*I beg you, Lord,
let the fiery, gentle power
of your love
take possession of my soul,
and snatch it away
from everything under heaven,
that I may die
for love of your love
as you saw fit to die
for love of mine.
Amen.*[15]

WEEK 16

Topic: Learn (Christlike)
Subtopic: Proclaim Freedom and Gospel
Verses: Luke 4:18-19 and Romans 1:16-17

In Luke 4:18-19, Jesus announces his mission: to proclaim good news to the poor, to proclaim freedom for the captives, and to restore sight to the blind. His mission is to set the oppressed free and to proclaim the year of the Lord's favor. We don't have our own mission; we join with Jesus in his mission. To be Christlike is to proclaim the gospel and the freedom of Christ and his Kingdom.

In 1 Corinthians 15:3-5, Paul defines the gospel in four parts: Christ died, Christ was buried, Christ was raised, and Christ appeared. Salvation is by grace through faith in him alone. As Scot McKnight says, the gospel is the story of Jesus completing the story of biblical Israel, for the sake of all humanity and all creation.[16] We imitate and follow Jesus by announcing this gospel of freedom, restoration, salvation, and *shalom*. We are not ashamed of this gospel. This gospel "is the power of God that brings salvation to everyone who believes" (Romans 1:16-17).

YOUR PLAN THIS WEEK

- Use Monday to read Luke 4:18-19 and Romans 1:16-17 in their context. Reflect on their meaning in context and how to live them out in your life, church, and neighborhood. Notice that both these passages are directed toward groups and their collective actions, not just individuals.

- Use Tuesday and Wednesday to memorize Luke 4:18-19, and use Thursday and Friday to memorize Romans 1:16-17. Use the weekend to practice the verses and to reflect on them.

- Take fifteen to twenty minutes each day to review the verses you've already learned. You may choose to write them down from memory. This will help ensure you don't forget them.

- Mark off the verses on the checklist once you've learned them.

- Work through the *Questions*, *Challenges*, and *Prayer* given below, alone or in a group. Modify them or add to them as you feel led by the Spirit.

QUESTIONS FOR MEDITATION AND GROUP REFLECTION

- During this week, how will you spend at least one period of the week learning Christ?

- Jesus describes his mission in Luke 4:18-19. How do we join with him in this mission?
- Why are some ashamed of the gospel? Are you? Why does Paul say he's not ashamed of the gospel (indeed, he is confident in its power)? (See Romans 1:16-17.)

CHALLENGES FOR YOU TO APPLY INDIVIDUALLY AND IN GROUPS

- Spend at least one period of the week learning Christ.
- Look at the words of Jesus in Luke 4:18-19, those of Paul in Romans 1:16-17, and read chapters 1 and 3 of *Keep Christianity Weird*. How is Jesus—through his gospel and example—calling you to pursue a weird, eccentric, and gospel-shaped life? Take some time to write down the ways you can live an eccentric life that honors the words (and passions) of Jesus and Paul in Luke 4:18-19 and Romans 1:16-17. Now, go and start living that way.
- Memorize Luke 4:18-19 and Romans 1:16-17.

A SAMPLE PRAYER

Lord Jesus, we pray for the nations of the world. We pray for your hand to be on the nations—bringing good governance, wise leadership, economic justice, political stability, and peace and justice and reconciliation. We pray that wars would end, ethnic hatreds would be tamed, politicians would provide ethical leadership, good governance would be restored, ecological restoration would start, global warming would halt, injustices would be righted, and poverty and disease would be reduced (and eventually eradicated).

We pray that you would be with those who suffer poverty and injustice. We pray for those who struggle each day to survive—afflicted by wars, poverty, injustices, and economic conditions beyond their control. Be with them, through your Spirit and in the actions of your church. Give them strength to meet each day and hope for a different future.

We pray that all nations and communities will hear the cries of the poor and respond with action to tackle poverty and its root causes. We pray for the people and groups campaigning for the eradication of poverty. Father, be with those who are seeking change to unjust social structures, flawed political systems, and harmful economic policies. Lord Jesus, we ask that governments, religious groups, NGOs, and other organizations would work together for fair trade, human rights, an end to debt, and other expressions of a just, prosperous, harmonious, compassionate, and happy society. We pray for the leaders of our government. Please give them the courage and conviction and passion to address poverty and injustice. Help them to advocate for the poor, to promote just policies, to resist self-interest and complacency, and to govern in righteous ways. Bless them with integrity and wisdom and courage. May they make wise and just choices for the good of all people.

Lord Jesus, you proclaim good news to the poor, freedom for the prisoners, and recovery of sight for the blind. You set the oppressed free and proclaim the year of the Lord's favor. Birth within us a passion and commitment to join you in this ministry.

Lord Jesus, we offer up the nations of the world to you. For yours is the kingdom, the power, and the glory forever. Amen.[17]

Habit 5: Sent (Missionary)

We see ourselves as sent by God to everywhere life takes us.

The fifth habit is identifying yourself as a missionary—a sent one. We'd like you to journal throughout the week all the ways you alerted others to the universal reign of God through Christ. This habit is about being missional. In *Surprise the World,* I (Michael) say that this involves living lives that proclaim the gospel and that alert others to God's reign of reconciliation, justice, beauty, and wholeness. This is about "reshaping our identities around our fundamental calling as the sent ones of God. . . . Remember that you can alert others to these things both by talking about them (witness) and by demonstrating them (action)."[18]

Check the box next to each verse after you've memorized it:

Be a Sent Community
☐ Matthew 28:18-20
☐ Acts 1:8

Pursue Justice
☐ Micah 6:8
☐ Isaiah 58:6-7

Be Incarnational and Present
☐ John 20:21
☐ Amos 5:24

Keep Christianity Weird
☐ 1 Peter 2:9
☐ Romans 12:1-2

WEEK 17

Topic: Sent (Missionary)
Subtopic: Be a Sent Community
Verses: Matthew 28:18-20 and Acts 1:8

Jesus' final words in Matthew are instructions to go and make disciples and a reassurance that he is with us in this mission. As we go and make disciples, we are instructed to baptize them, teaching them to obey the words of Jesus. "And surely I am with you always, to the very end of the age" (Matthew 28:18-20). We are a sent community, joining with

Jesus in his mission in the world. David Bosch defines mission as "quite simply, the participation of Christians in the liberating mission of Jesus, wagering on a future that verifiable experience seems to belie. It is the good news of God's love, incarnated in the witness of a community, for the sake of the world."[19] We don't have our own mission, and we don't do mission in our own strength. It is God's mission. And he gives us power in the Holy Spirit to be "witnesses in Jerusalem, and in all Judea and Samaria, and to the ends of the earth" (Acts 1:8).

YOUR PLAN THIS WEEK

- Use Monday to read Matthew 28:18-20 and Acts 1:8 in their context. Reflect on their meaning in context and how to live them out in your life, church, and neighborhood. Notice that both these passages are directed toward groups and their collective actions, not just individuals.

- Use Tuesday and Wednesday to memorize Matthew 28:18-20, and use Thursday and Friday to memorize Acts 1:8. Use the weekend to practice the verses and to reflect on them.

- Take fifteen to twenty minutes each day to review the verses you've already learned. You may choose to write them down from memory. This will help ensure you don't forget them.

- Mark off the verses on the checklist once you've learned them.

- Work through the *Questions*, *Challenges*, and *Prayer* given below, alone or in a group. Modify them or add to them as you feel led by the Spirit.

QUESTIONS FOR MEDITATION AND GROUP REFLECTION

- During this week, how will you alert others to the universal reign of God through Christ?
- Why does Jesus make discipleship the heart of the Great Commission?

- In Matthew 28:18-20, we see references to sentness, obedience, passing on the message of Jesus, baptism, and making more disciples. How do all these things relate to being a sent community?
- Why does Jesus begin the Great Commission by talking about his authority and then end it by assuring them of his presence? How do these things help us as a sent community?
- Why are the power and presence of the Holy Spirit necessary for boldness and effectiveness in witness (see Acts 1:8)?
- What are Judea, Samaria, and the ends of the earth to Christians in your culture (i.e., your neighborhood, city, state, country, region)? How are you obeying the Great Commission?
- What does it mean to be a "witness"? How are you being a witness?

CHALLENGES FOR YOU TO APPLY INDIVIDUALLY AND IN GROUPS

- Journal throughout the week all the ways you alerted others to the universal reign of God through Christ.
- Discuss the missional priorities in *Surprise the World* chapter 7—reconciliation, justice, beauty, and wholeness. Talk about how you can practice at least one of these together in your neighborhood or city over the next few months.
- What are some practical ways you can announce reconciliation (champion it, describe it, and advocate for it) and show reconciliation (be reconciled to others and help broker reconciliation among others) this year?
- Memorize Matthew 28:18-20 and Acts 1:8.

A SAMPLE PRAYER

Father, fill us with a passion to make disciples of all nations, baptizing them in the name of the Father and of the Son and of the Holy Spirit, and teaching them to obey everything commanded by Jesus, our Lord.

You are with us always, to the very end of the age.

Come upon us with your Spirit in power, that we might be witnesses in our neighborhoods, cities, nations, and to the ends of the earth.

Grant us the ability to pray in the Spirit on all occasions with all kinds of prayers and requests.

Enable us to be alert and to always keep on praying for all the Lord's people.

We pray for those who proclaim the gospel in word and deed, that whenever they speak, words may be given them so that they will fearlessly make known the mystery of the gospel, for which many are ambassadors in chains.

We pray that they and we may declare it fearlessly, as we should.

Amen.[20]

WEEK 18

Topic: Sent (Missionary)
Subtopic: Pursue Justice
Verses: Micah 6:8 and Isaiah 58:6-7

Jesus calls his church to prioritize the elimination of poverty, injustice, and greed and to name and confront structural sin in the church and in the world. This means "to act justly and to love mercy and to walk humbly with your God" (Micah 6:8). The Bible shows us that God cares deeply about social justice, and he calls his people to act justly and work toward a just society. Churches that follow God's commands to seek justice and mercy are merely joining with Jesus in his mission. Their prophetic and activistic lifestyles are simply forms of obedience to the Great Commission and to the witness of verses like Micah 6:8 and Isaiah 58:6-7. A missional church is a church that pursues mercy, liberation, compassion, welcome, justice, and the gospel of peace and salvation.

YOUR PLAN THIS WEEK

- Use Monday to read Micah 6:8 and Isaiah 58:6-7 in their context. Reflect on their meaning in context and how to live them out in your life, church, and neighborhood. Notice that both these passages are directed toward groups and their collective actions, not just individuals.

- Use Tuesday and Wednesday to memorize Micah 6:8, and use Thursday and Friday to memorize Isaiah 58:6-7. Use the weekend to practice the verses and to reflect on them.

- Take fifteen to twenty minutes each day to review the verses you've already learned. You may choose to write them down from memory. This will help ensure you don't forget them.

- Mark off the verses on the checklist once you've learned them.

- Work through the *Questions, Challenges,* and *Prayer* given below, alone or in a group. Modify them or add to them as you feel led by the Spirit.

QUESTIONS FOR MEDITATION AND GROUP REFLECTION

- During this week, how will you alert others to the universal reign of God through Christ?
- What is the difference between mercy and justice? Why do we need to put our energy into both?
- Micah 6:8 in the original language begins with a focus on mortality—where some translations render the verse "O man" or "O people," the Hebrew translates literally to "O mortal." Why does Micah 6:8 start with a focus on our mortality? How do "god complexes" (an inflated sense of our ability and importance) prevent us from doing justice and showing mercy? How does humbly accepting our limitations and depending on God's greatness strengthen our efforts toward mercy and justice?

- Isaiah 58:6-7 says that the kind of spirituality that pleases God includes addressing injustice; freeing those in bondage; sharing with those in need; and welcoming the stranger, the homeless, and the displaced. Why are these things important to God? How do they reflect his character and actions?

CHALLENGES FOR YOU TO APPLY INDIVIDUALLY AND IN GROUPS

- Journal throughout the week all the ways you alerted others to the universal reign of God through Christ.
- In a small group, read Isaiah 1:16-17; Isaiah 58; Isaiah 61:1-3; Amos 5; Micah 6:8; Matthew 25:31-46; and Luke 4:14-21. As you read through these verses, take notes together on how acts of advocacy and solidarity and the pursuit of justice fit into a properly understood gospel.
- Spend an evening writing prayers about justice (personally or in a group). If it assists, use the words of Micah 6 and Isaiah 58 to help you write these prayers (but don't feel limited to the words of those verses).
- Write five things you will do (personally and together) to address injustice in your neighborhood or city. Hold each other accountable to do these things.
- Pick an issue of injustice or some social concern in your community, and then research gatherings you could attend to help you be more knowledgeable and equipped to address it in your context.
- Memorize Micah 6:8 and Isaiah 58:6-7.

A SAMPLE PRAYER

Lord, give us a passion to do justice, love mercy, and walk humbly with our God.

Help us to be transformed nonconformists who offer our bodies as living sacrifices to God as our true and proper act of worship.

May we refuse conformity to the values, pressures, antagonisms, ideologies, and powers of this world and, instead, be transformed by the renewing of our minds.

May we replace war with peace, pride with humility, hate with love, selfishness with self-sacrifice, lies with truth, materialism with simplicity, individualism with community, and inequality and exploitation with equality and justice. May we replace idolatry with true worship, ambition with contentment, anxiety with trust, grasping with receiving, competition with collaboration, division with unity, conflict with shalom, exclusion with embrace, and antagonism with compassion, service, and love.

Help us to loosen the chains of injustice, untie the cords of the yoke, set the oppressed free, break every yoke, share food with the hungry, provide the poor wanderer with shelter, clothe the naked, do away with the yoke of oppression, and care for the oppressed.

Then our light will break forth like the dawn, and our healing will quickly appear. Then we will call, and you will answer us; we will cry for help, and you will respond.

Give us a fresh desire and commitment to protect the weak, care for the poor and hungry, nurture creation, honor different races and cultures, value women and children, build peace with justice, and pursue justice with mercy, humility, and love.

Yours is the kingdom, the power, and the glory, forever. Amen.[21]

WEEK 19

Topic: Sent (Missionary)
Subtopic: Be Incarnational and Present
Verses: John 20:21 and Amos 5:24

Describing the themes in my book *Incarnate*, I (Michael) say the following:

The story of Christianity is a story of incarnation—God taking on flesh and dwelling among the people he created. God appointing and sending people as his body, his hands and feet. Disciples of Jesus bearing the good news even as they bear the marks of his passion. Whatever Christianity is, it is at least a matter of flesh and blood and the ends of the earth.[22]

Jesus doesn't tell us to escape or avoid the world. Jesus sends us into the world. He entered its joy and pain, beauty and mess, laughter and sorrow, pleasures and sufferings; and he calls us to do the same. "As the Father has sent me, I am sending you" (John 20:21). We want to see "justice roll on like a river," and we want the world to be filled with peace, reconciliation, righteousness, and love (Amos 5:24). But that only happens (or at least begins) when we are present and engaged in our neighborhoods and communities (see the prayer this week by Lauren Lai). Our religious festivals and rituals mean nothing if we aren't present in our neighborhoods, being on local and incarnational mission and finding small, homegrown, local ways we can help "justice roll on like a river" (Amos 5:21-24).

YOUR PLAN THIS WEEK

- Use Monday to read John 20:21 and Amos 5:24 in their context. Reflect on their meaning in context and how to live them out in your life, church, and neighborhood. Notice that both these verses are directed toward groups and their collective actions, not just individuals.

- Use Tuesday and Wednesday to memorize John 20:21, and use Thursday and Friday to memorize Amos 5:24. Use the weekend to practice the verses and to reflect on them.

- Take fifteen to twenty minutes each day to review the verses you've already learned. You may choose to write them down from memory. This will help ensure you don't forget them.

- Mark off the verses on the checklist once you've learned them.

- Work through the *Questions*, *Challenges*, and *Prayer* given below, alone or in a group. Modify them or add to them as you feel led by the Spirit.

QUESTIONS FOR MEDITATION AND GROUP REFLECTION

- During this week, how will you alert others to the universal reign of God through Christ?
- Jesus says, "Peace be with you! As the Father has sent me, I am sending you" (John 20:21). What does he mean? How do we go into the world (incarnationally) the way Jesus did?
- Reflect on the following words by Darrell Guder. What does he tell us incarnational mission and ministry involve?

In the incarnation of Jesus Christ, God revealed himself as the One who is *with and for* his creation. Now, as the Risen Lord sends his Spirit to empower the church, *we are called to become God's people present in the world, with and for the world*, like St. John pointing always to Christ. The most incarnational dimension of our witness is defined by the cross itself, as we experience with Jesus that bearing his cross transforms our suffering into witness.

Incarnational witness is, therefore, a way of describing Christian vocation in terms of Jesus Christ as the messenger, the message, and *the model for all who follow after him*. To speak of the incarnation missionally is to *link who Jesus was, what Jesus did, and how he did it, in one great event that defines all that it means to be Christian.*[23]

- How do we follow Christ's example of humility, of suffering for the sake of others, of identifying with sinful and wounded people, and of making himself nothing for the sake of God's redemptive purposes?

CHALLENGES FOR YOU TO APPLY INDIVIDUALLY AND IN GROUPS

- Journal throughout the week all the ways you alerted others to the universal reign of God through Christ.
- In your small group, brainstorm ways God is calling your group to serve among the suffering, hurting, sinful, marginalized, addicted, hostile, excluded, unbelieving, rejected, or displaced (choose one or two of these groups). Then explore together how you will seek to serve among this group in practical ways over the next few months.
- There are many groups that Christians (and others) often feel afraid of. These include strangers, foreigners, perceived "enemies," undocumented immigrants, those of no professed faith, and those of other faiths. In your small group, do the following: First, choose one of these groups. Second, brainstorm how you can get to know people from this group in practical, open, humble, and relational ways. Finally, make commitments and plans to do that together.
- In your small group or ministry leadership team, write down some responses to the following: "What are some practical ways your group or church can move from *being with* marginalized people to *serving with* them and also allowing them to serve and minister to you?" Now make some commitments to follow through on those actions.
- Memorize John 20:21 and Amos 5:24.

A SAMPLE PRAYER

Our Lord, our God,
You call us to be salt and light. Salt and light . . . what
does that even mean? You call us to be different, to stand out.
And as we look around us and see conflict, hatred, violence,
racism, ridicule and oppression—and not just in other countries,

but within the very borders of our own country, within our neighborhoods—surely it should be easy for us to stand out, to be different, to be light.

Yet sometimes I fear that we mold ourselves to fit the society around us and the culture we live in. And that our "salt and light," our difference, is that on a Sunday morning we walk into a building and sing some songs and listen to a talk, and that on a weeknight evening we go to someone's house and read some words from the Bible. And I say that not to mock what we do, but to question whether our difference is about the places that we go, rather than our hearts and the love that we show.

Lord God, I pray that we don't relegate "justice" to a sermon series, or as being "over there," or as "someone else's calling," or as "us helping them," but rather embrace it as being part and parcel, inherent, in us as God's people.

"Let justice roll down like waters"—do we picture grand waterfalls, a knight on a white horse, a hero saving the lost? Or do we picture ourselves in a conversation with a coworker or a friend or at a party, where we speak up against an ignorant or prejudiced comment? Do we picture ourselves in a place beyond our leafy suburbs, perhaps a place that makes us feel a bit uncomfortable? Do we picture ourselves going beyond our interests and looking to the interests of others?

We pride ourselves on not being the perpetrator, yet we see no problem in being the bystander. But a bystander cannot be salt; they cannot be light.

I pray that we stand when we should stand, speak out when we can speak out, be generous when there is need, and show compassion always.

Yet may we not have the mindset that we need to help "them," that we are doing good for those "poor people." Instead, may we see others as our fellow humans, with all the dignity that every person has. For the brokenness that people experience does not make them any less whole. While we may be more privileged by virtue of our circumstances, we are no more superior.

"Let justice roll down like waters"—let us not plaster that on posters or declare it in song until we are willing and committed to find what justice means in each of our lives, lest we empty those bold words of their meaning. And it doesn't have to be a massive act; it could be a small moment or a passing interaction, for while injustice is everywhere, through Jesus' love, justice too can be everywhere.

I pray that we will be willing to have the uncomfortable conversation, to go to the uncomfortable place, to be uncomfortable people—because perhaps only then can we be salt and light.

Lord God, I ask that you, working through us, would make our neighborhoods, our city, our country, our world more like heaven on earth, until Jesus returns, when justice will truly roll down like waters, and righteousness like an ever-flowing stream.

In Jesus' almighty name,
Amen.[24]

WEEK 20

Topic: Sent (Missionary)
Subtopic: Keep Christianity Weird
Verses: 1 Peter 2:9 and Romans 12:1-2

Jesus was weird.

He was a homeless, unmarried, thirtysomething rabbi who recruited a bunch of young (some still in their teens), uneducated boys to hit the road with him, preaching the coming of the Kingdom and calling on people to repent of their sins.

He didn't mince words. He told the truth, even when it made people hate him. Especially when it made powerful people hate him.

He fraternized with prostitutes, extortionists, collaborators, zealots, and those euphemistically referred to as "sinners"— ordinary, irreligious people.[25]

Jesus' church has sought to be safe, conventional, and socially acceptable for too long. We need to recover our weirdness, eccentricity, and difference if we are going to join Jesus in discipleship and mission. First Peter 2:9 tells us that we aren't a people of this world anymore; we are a people born of the Spirit, a chosen and "peculiar people" (KJV). As the Spirit changes our hearts, as the Scriptures renew our minds, and as we offer our bodies as living sacrifices, we become transformed nonconformists (Romans 12:1-2).

Martin Luther King Jr. once wrote:

> This hour in history needs a dedicated circle of transformed nonconformists. Our planet teeters on the brink of atomic annihilation; dangerous passions of pride, hatred, and selfishness are enthroned in our lives; truth lies prostrate on the rugged hills of nameless Calvaries; and [people] do reverence before false gods of nationalism and materialism. The saving of our world from pending doom will come, not through the complacent adjustment of the conforming majority, but through the creative maladjustment of a nonconforming minority.[26]

We pray for the courage and grace to be weird, peculiar, creatively maladjusted, missional disciples. This is what it means to follow Jesus in discipleship and mission.

YOUR PLAN THIS WEEK

- Use Monday to read 1 Peter 2:9 and Romans 12:1-2 in their context. Reflect on their meaning in context and how to live them out in your life, church, and neighborhood. Notice that both these passages are directed toward groups and their collective actions, not just individuals.

- Use Tuesday and Wednesday to memorize 1 Peter 2:9, and use Thursday and Friday to memorize Romans 12:1-2. Use the weekend to practice the verses and to reflect on them.

- Take fifteen to twenty minutes each day to review the verses you've already learned. You may choose to write them down from memory. This will help ensure you don't forget them.

- Mark off the verses on the checklist once you've learned the verses.

- Work through the *Questions, Challenges,* and *Prayer* given below, alone or in a group. Modify them or add to them as you feel led by the Spirit.

QUESTIONS FOR MEDITATION AND GROUP REFLECTION

- During this week, how will you alert others to the universal reign of God through Christ?

- "When I call on you to keep Christianity weird, I'm asking you to reject materialism, foster community, promote diversity, share resources, protect the environment, start ethical businesses, feed the hungry, play beautiful music, bring peace and joy and life back to our cities."[27] Why are these things weird? How is Jesus inspiring you to keep your faith and discipleship weird?

- How do we live in a way that affirms God's presence in the world *and* contrasts those values or behaviors that are divisive and destructive and sinful in the world? Why do we need to *both* affirm God's presence in the world *and* contrast many of the ways of the world to be truly weird?

CHALLENGES FOR YOU TO APPLY INDIVIDUALLY AND IN GROUPS

- Journal throughout the week all the ways you alerted others to the universal reign of God through Christ.

- List some everyday and practical ways you can resist the draw to "conform to the pattern of this world" and instead be "transformed by the renewing of your mind" (Romans 12:1-2). What will you seek to reject (materialism, consumerism, prejudice, conflict, racism, sexism, etc.) *and* what will you seek to embrace (simplicity, generosity, welcome, love, honor, etc.)?

- In your ministry team or small group, write a list of some Christians that have inspired you by the weirdness and passion of their faith and witness. Then discuss what inspired you about their lives and also how you will live these things out in your own lives, individually and together.
- Memorize 1 Peter 2:9 and Romans 12:1-2.

A SAMPLE PRAYER:

Grant us the grace to be unusual and weird:
  To resist being molded by the world,
  to refuse complacency,
  to see the world differently than the world sees itself,
  to be eccentric—off center, unique, different, and unconventional,
  to not conform to the patterns of the world
  but to be transformed by the renewal of our minds.
Help us to be dissatisfied by sin and conformity to the world.
Enable us to be conformed to the image of Jesus Christ.
Grant us the strength and courage to resist the allure of acceptability,
  to get back to the unsafe roots of our faith.
  to be equipped to surprise the world with the Good News of Jesus.
  to challenge the way things are
  by living a life that has been truly set free by Christ.
Give us boldness to keep Christianity weird and to be transformed
  nonconformists,
through Jesus Christ our Lord,
Amen.

6

freedom on the other side of regulation

Few things are sadder than encountering a person who knows exactly what he should do, yet cannot muster enough energy to do it.

MIHALY CSIKSZENTMIHALYI

Hank Azaria is one of the world's most successful voice actors. He's best known for his work on the animated series *The Simpsons*, voicing such characters as Moe the bar owner, Chief Wiggum, the Comic Book Guy, and most controversially, Kwik-E-Mart proprietor Apu.

He's also been in a ton of movies and television series. In many of them, he has affected a funny voice to add humor to the role. His costars and directors are regularly astonished at his freakish ability to mimic any voice he hears.

Interestingly, his entry into acting was almost by accident. He just started memorizing his favorite comedians' routines for his friends' amusement:

I was a huge fan of comedy and movies and TV growing up, and I was able to memorize and mimic a lot of things, not realizing that that meant I probably wanted to be an

135

actor. I just really, really amused myself and my friends with memorizing entire George Carlin or Steve Martin albums, or mimicking whatever we saw on *Happy Days* the night before, or whatever, not realizing that kind of obsessive ability to mimic things meant that I probably had an affinity for acting.[1]

The process of memorization unleashed an untapped skill, a lifelong vocation for him. But Azaria's isn't an isolated case. The greats in just about any sphere of the creative arts started out by doing the laborious work of memorization. If you ever get to visit the Van Gogh Museum in Amsterdam, you can go to a room where all of Vincent's early drawings are stored in huge pull-out drawers. There you'll find scores of pictures of hands or feet, drawn in great detail by the young Van Gogh. He spent his early years as an art student learning the basic techniques by heart before he even considered branching out to paint *The Starry Night*.

Likewise, jazz great John Coltrane memorized and rehearsed scales and arpeggios incessantly so that he could revolutionize jazz music. At age seventeen he got his first saxophone, an alto, and set about practically memorizing Nicolas Slonimsky's *Thesaurus of Scales and Melodic Patterns*. He imitated the greats like Charlie Parker, Lester Young, and Coleman Hawkins. He practiced continuously. Later, he could compose great music in the very act of playing it before a live audience. But he never stopped practicing—up to four hours a day, according to Coltrane himself (his wife groused it was more like ten!).

We know that piano practice was torture for many of you when you were young. If your heart's not in it, it can become like a prison. But Coltrane and others, who loved their craft, gave every spare minute to practice. Virtuoso violinist Yehudi Menuhin once said of practice and memorization: "Practicing is not forced labor; it is a refined art that partakes of intuition, of inspiration, patience, elegance, clarity, balance, and, above all, the search for ever greater joy in movement and expression."[2]

For the Christian, studying and memorizing the Bible should be an obsession at least equal to jazz music for Coltrane or comedy routines for Hank Azaria. But the Christian needs to keep a posture of submission to God's Word at the heart of Scripture memorization. Just as Olympic athletes train incessantly so their bodies know instinctually what to do in actual competition, so Scripture memorization informs our missional instincts so that we live habitually as ambassadors of the Kingdom whenever the opportunity presents itself.

As we look through the pages of history, we see how reading, memorizing, and applying the Bible transformed the lives of ordinary people and freed them to embrace the path of activism and radical discipleship.

Catherine Booth is a striking example. Having founded the Salvation Army with her husband, William, she testified to the pivotal role Scripture played in her faith and activist lifestyle. Catherine's ministry was extraordinary. She visited and cared for people in the slums and provided food and clothing for children and families in need. She established shelters for homeless people and helped the Salvation Army set up a factory for low-paid workers with better pay and conditions. She campaigned against the use of cancer-causing chemicals and against what amounted to modern-day slavery. She helped people find employment and worked to better the lives of drug addicts and alcoholics. Catherine sought freedom and dignity for prostitutes and campaigned against the abuse of women and children. She spoke up for gender equality and advocated for the right for women to preach and teach. Catherine was a revivalist, social reformer, cofounder of a radical Christian movement, political activist, gospel preacher, and champion of women's rights.

Catherine Booth's devotional practices are well known, and she often spoke about how the words of the Bible inspired her to embrace a life committed to God's truth, freedom, and justice. Even though Catherine received only two years of formal schooling, she had "read the sacred Book from cover to cover eight times through" before she was twelve.[3]

Her enthusiasm for the Bible only increased as she went through her teens. When she was eighteen, Catherine wrote,

Above all, I am determined to search the Scriptures more attentively, for in them I have eternal life. I have read my Bible through twice during the last sixteen months, but I must read it with more prayer for light and understanding. Oh, may it be my meat and drink! May I meditate on it day and night! And then I shall "bring forth fruit in season, my leaf also shall not wither, and whatsoever I do shall prosper."[4]

In her mature years of ministry, Catherine would speak of her passion for the Bible and for learning and memorizing it. She made it clear to everyone who would listen that it was the words of Jesus and the Bible that fueled and empowered her passion for social reform, spiritual revival, and women's rights.

What we take from Catherine Booth's example is the need for Christians to do the simple, straightforward, hard work of prioritizing what's most important to them. The key is to find the freedom on the other side of regulation. If Bible memorization is just a deathly rule to keep, you won't stick with it. But long-term commitment to practice eventually leads to the breakthrough of finding freedom in the routine.

Retired Navy SEAL Jocko Willink is a big believer in getting up early. Willink has written some bestselling motivational books based on lessons he learned during his stellar military career, and rising at 4:30 a.m. is one of his core disciplines. Recently, when asked about his personal daily regime, he replied, "No one wants to hear this, but step number one is to wake up early. That is where it starts. It does take discipline to get out of bed early, but that sets the tone and the pattern of discipline for the rest of the day."[5]

Jocko Willink's most recent book is titled *Discipline Equals Freedom*, and he describes their relationship this way:

While discipline and freedom seem like they sit on opposite sides of the spectrum, they are actually very connected.

Freedom is what everyone wants—to be able to act and live

with freedom. But the only way to get to a place of freedom is through discipline. If you want financial freedom, you have to have financial discipline. If you want more free time, you have to follow a more disciplined time management system. You also have to have the discipline to say "No" to things that eat up your time with no payback—things like random YouTube videos, click-bait on the internet, and even events that you agree to attend when you know you won't want to be there. [The concept that] discipline equals freedom applies to every aspect of life: if you want more freedom, get more discipline.[6]

Canadian psychology professor Jordan B. Peterson couldn't agree more. In his oft-quoted appearance on Joe Rogan's podcast, Peterson pointed out how annoyed he gets by young people who want to change the world when they can't even clean up their own bedrooms. He groused:

Don't be fixing up the economy, eighteen-year-olds. You don't know anything about the economy. It's a massive complex machine beyond anyone's understanding and you mess with at your peril. So can you even clean up your own room? No. Well you think about that. You should think about that, because if you can't even clean up your own room, who . . . are you to give advice to the world?[7]

He's got a point. It's not that a clean room is the answer to the world's problems, but a person who can order their own private world is more likely to make an impact on the rest of society. This echoes the wisdom of Confucius, who said,

To put the world in order, we must first put the nation in order; to put the nation in order, we must put the family in order; to put the family in order, we must cultivate our personal life; and to cultivate our personal life, we must first set our hearts right.[8]

Our advice is to start small. Begin by submitting yourself to memorize the passages we listed in chapter 5. Show that you can be trusted with this task and then allow those verses—all of which are calling you to love and serve the Lord and others—to shape your outlook. And then the action will proceed. Then the world can be put in order.

The *Kingdom Impact Memory System* integrates memorizing with reading, reflection, prayer, relationships, and action. This is because we believe that memory is a foundation not only for character and identity but also for action and mission. In this way we surprise the world, keep Christianity weird, and help to heal a broken humanity.

The Bible prioritizes memory. God calls his people to remember throughout the pages of the Bible. Remember that you were once slaves, and God brought you up out of Egypt (Deuteronomy 6:12). Remember the wonders God has done, his miracles and judgments (1 Chronicles 16:12-13). Remember the Lord your God, who blesses you and keeps his covenant promise to bless his children (Deuteronomy 8:18). "Remember your Creator in the days of your youth" (Ecclesiastes 12:1). Remember Jesus Christ and all he's done: "This is my body, which is for you; do this in remembrance of me" (1 Corinthians 11:24). Remember that you were once separated from Christ, excluded from Israel's covenant, without hope and without God in the world. Remember that you have been reconciled through Christ, who is your peace and who made you fellow citizens of his household (Ephesians 2:11-22). This list goes on and on, right across the pages of the Old and New Testaments.

When you read through Psalm 119, you get a sense of the psalmist's passion for the Word of God. This hunger for God and his Word—and constant marinating in God's words—transforms his character and leads him into action. God's Word makes him steadfast in trial, resilient under persecution, passionate for the Lord, and countercultural in outlook and action. Memorizing and obeying the Bible does that. The final words of Psalm 119 are, notably, "Seek your servant, for I have not forgotten your commands" (verse 176).

To remember is, at its essence, to not forget. We don't choose all our memories, but we do choose some. And when we commit to memory the commands of God, the teachings of Christ, the story of God's people, the promises of God's vision for us and for the world, and the testament to God's faithfulness that pervade the Scriptures, we are shaped by these chosen memories into people who will follow God to the ends of the earth, bringing God's Good News with them. We find ourselves committed to and capable of the kind of radical action in the world that can only come from God and gives glory to God alone.

the memory verse checklist

Check the box next to each verse after you've memorized it.

Habit 1: Bless

Affirm and Honor Others
☐ 1 Thessalonians 5:11
☐ Galatians 3:26-28

Release Finances
☐ Matthew 6:19-21, 24
☐ Matthew 6:2-4

Exhibit Practical Giving
☐ 1 John 3:17-18
☐ 2 Corinthians 8:7

Commit to Prayer
☐ 1 Timothy 2:1-2
☐ Jeremiah 29:7

Habit 2: Eat

Welcome Refugees and Immigrants
☐ Matthew 25:35-36, 40
☐ Deuteronomy 10:18-19

Show Hospitality and Welcome
☐ Luke 14:13-14
☐ Hebrews 13:2

Enjoy Table Fellowship
☐ Luke 7:34-35
☐ Luke 24:30-31

Show Justice, Mercy, Compassion
☐ Zechariah 7:9-10
☐ James 2:15-17

Habit 3: Listen

Repent and Lament
☐ Acts 3:19-20
☐ Joel 2:12-13

Be Peacemakers
☐ Matthew 5:9
☐ Romans 12:14, 18

Seek Guidance and Direction
☐ Psalm 25:4-5
☐ Proverbs 2:6-9

Be Disciplined and Corrected
☐ Hebrews 12:7-8, 11
☐ Revelation 3:19

Habit 4: Learn

Love God, Neighbors, and
Enemies
☐ Mark 12:30-31
☐ Matthew 5:43-46

Seek Reconciliation
☐ 2 Corinthians 5:18
☐ Colossians 1:19-20

Display Humility and
Self-Sacrifice
☐ Philippians 2:3-4
☐ Matthew 16:24-25

Proclaim Freedom and Gospel
☐ Luke 4:18-19
☐ Romans 1:16-17

Habit 5: Sent

Be a Sent Community
☐ Matthew 28:18-20
☐ Acts 1:8

Pursue Justice
☐ Micah 6:8
☐ Isaiah 58:6-7

Be Incarnational and Present
☐ John 20:21
☐ Amos 5:24

Keep Christianity Weird
☐ 1 Peter 2:9
☐ Romans 12:1-2

memorize the sermon on the mount in 24 or 48 months

Here's a method and plan for memorizing the Sermon on the Mount (Matthew 5–7) in twenty-four or forty-eight months. It's a guide, so if it takes longer that's fine. This memorization of the Sermon on the Mount is in addition to the verses in our memory system, for those who want to challenge themselves further.

Here and there you'll be given a "revision month," which is a month with fewer new verses to memorize, giving you an opportunity to review and correct any mistakes in your memorization so far.

In case you choose to memorize as a group, we've suggested a monthly theme for group study and service and mission. You will need to write the weekly small group study questions, but the themes line up with what you are memorizing from Matthew 5–7. The words of Jesus in the Sermon on the Mount have the power to transform our personal lives and also our lives together and in the world.

Month 1 (or Months 1 and 2)

Topic: The Beatitudes Part A
Verses: Matthew 5:1-5
Small group theme this month: The ethics of Jesus
Your plan this month: Memorize these five verses.
- **Reflection:** How will you live out the ethics and qualities described among those who are "blessed"?

Month 2 (or Months 3 and 4)

Topic: The Beatitudes Part B
Verses: Matthew 5:6-10
Small group theme this month: Peacemaking and hungering for righteousness
Your plan this month: Memorize these five verses.
- **Reflection:** How will you live out the ethics and qualities described among those who are "blessed"?

Month 3 (or Months 5 and 6)

Topic: Salt, Light, and a City on a Hill
Verses: Matthew 5:11-16
Small group theme this month: Good public deeds that glorify God
Your plan this month: Memorize these six verses.
- **Reflection:** What does it mean to be salt and light and a city on a hill?

Month 4 (or Months 7 and 8)

Topic: Law and Righteousness
Verses: Matthew 5:17-20
Small group theme this month: Practicing and following Jesus' commands

Your plan this month: Memorize these four verses.

- **Reflection:** How do we more fully practice and teach Jesus' commands? What does it mean to have a righteousness that surpasses the righteousness that is often displayed by religious leaders?

Month 5 (or Months 9 and 10)

Topic: Anger and Reconciliation
Verses: Matthew 5:21-26
Small group theme this month: Forgiveness and reconciliation
Your plan this month: Memorize these six verses.

- **Reflection:** Who do you need to be reconciled to? How can you be someone who promotes reconciliation in the world?

Month 6 (or Months 11 and 12)

Topic: Lust, Relinquishment, and Desire
Verses: Matthew 5:27-30
Small group theme this month: Christian integrity—thinking about lust, desire, integrity, and relinquishment
Your plan this month: Memorize these four verses.

- **Reflection:** Have you given in to lust? What do you desire? What are you doing to let go of lust and to have your desires transformed, with the help of God?

Month 7 (or Months 13 and 14)

Topic: Divorce and Caring for Others
Verses: Matthew 5:31-32
Small group theme this month: Fidelity, faithfulness, and caring for others
Your plan this month: Memorize these two verses.

- **Reflection:** How are you practicing faithfulness and consideration of the needs of others? How are you replacing infidelity and selfishness with fidelity and selflessness?

Revision Month: There are only two verses this month, so make this month especially about revision. Go through what you've learned so far, and revise and practice. This consolidates your learning and your Bible memorization.

Month 8 (or Months 15 and 16)

Topic: Saying "Yes" and "No"
Verses: Matthew 5:33-37
Small group theme this month: Simply saying "yes" and "no"
Your plan this month: Memorize these five verses.
- **Reflection:** Are you being a person of integrity and being true to your word?

Month 9 (or Months 17 and 18)

Topic: Turning the Other Cheek
Verses: Matthew 5:38-42
Small group theme this month: Forgiveness, peacemaking, and turning the other cheek
Your plan this month: Memorize these five verses.
- **Reflection:** What does it mean to turn the other cheek today in a world full of conflict, animosity, and antagonism?

Month 10 (or Months 19 and 20)

Topic: Loving Our Enemies
Verses: Matthew 5:43-48
Small group theme this month: Loving and praying for enemies

Your plan this month: Memorize these six verses.

- **Reflection:** Who is your neighbor? Who is your enemy? How are you loving and praying for your neighbor and your enemy?

Month 11 (or Months 21 and 22)

Topic: Humility and Generosity
Verses: Matthew 6:1-4
Small group theme this month: Being generous, with humility
Your plan this month: Memorize these four verses.

- **Reflection:** Who are the needy in your neighborhood and society? How are you caring for them, especially in a secret and unnoticed way?

Month 12 (or Months 23 and 24)

Topic: Prayer
Verses: Matthew 6:5-8
Small group theme this month: Learning to pray
Your plan this month: Memorize these four verses.

- **Reflection:** Are you setting aside time each day for secret, personal prayer, where you grow your intimacy with God?

Month 13 (or Months 25 and 26)

Topic: The Lord's Prayer
Verses: Matthew 6:9-15
Small group theme this month: Praying and living out the Lord's Prayer
Your plan this month: Memorize these seven verses.

- **Reflection:** How are the words of this prayer shaping your heart and life? Who do you need to forgive, and how are you moving toward forgiveness?

Month 14 (or Months 27 and 28)

Topic: Fasting and Humility
Verses: Matthew 6:16-18
Small group theme this month: Spiritual practices, exercised with humility
Your plan this month: Memorize these three verses.
- **Reflection:** What things in your life have become idols or indulgences, and when will you fast from them? How are you seeking to imitate Christ's humility?

Revision Month: There are only three verses this month, so make this month especially about revision. Go through what you've learned so far, and revise and practice. This consolidates your learning and your Bible memorization.

Month 15 (or Months 29 and 30)

Topic: Storing Treasures in Heaven
Verses: Matthew 6:19-24
Small group theme this month: Treasures in heaven and serving God and not money
Your plan this month: Memorize these six verses.
- **Reflection:** What do you treasure and desire? Are you trying to serve two masters?

Month 16 (or Months 31 and 32)

Topic: Worry and Trust
Verses: Matthew 6:25-29
Small group theme this month: Trusting God
Your plan this month: Memorize these five verses.
- **Reflection:** Are you moving from worry to trust, from anxiety to peace, and from busyness to rest?

Month 17 (or Months 33 and 34)

Topic: Seeking God's Kingdom First
Verses: Matthew 6:30-34
Small group theme this month: Seeking first God's Kingdom and his righteousness
Your plan this month: Memorize these five verses.

- **Reflection:** Are you seeking God's Kingdom and righteousness before all other things? How is this expressed in your life?

Month 18 (or Months 35 and 36)

Topic: Don't Judge Others
Verses: Matthew 7:1-6
Small group theme this month: Stop judging others
Your plan this month: Memorize these six verses.

- **Reflection:** How are you letting go of exclusion and judgmentalism and, instead, embracing acceptance, inclusion, and grace?

Month 19 (or Months 37 and 38)

Topic: Ask, Seek, Knock
Verses: Matthew 7:7-12
Small group theme this month: Seeking God expectantly
Your plan this month: Memorize these six verses.

- **Reflection:** Are you approaching God—asking, seeking, and knocking—with expectation? Are you doing to others what you would have them do to you?

Month 20 (or Months 39 and 40)

Topic: The Small Gate and Narrow Road
Verses: Matthew 7:13-14

Small group theme this month: The narrow way of discipleship

Your plan this month: Memorize these two verses.

- **Reflection:** What do these verses mean? How are you choosing the small gate and narrow road instead of the wide gate and broad road?

Revision Month: There are only two verses this month, so make this month especially about revision. Go through what you've learned so far, and revise and practice. This consolidates your learning and your Bible memorization.

Month 21 (or Months 41 and 42)

Topic: Bearing Good Fruit

Verses: Matthew 7:15-20

Small group theme this month: Bearing good fruit

Your plan this month: Memorize these six verses.

- **Reflection:** Are you bearing good fruit? How is that expressed through peacemaking, reconciliation, justice seeking, faith sharing, missional witness, and activist spirituality?

Month 22 (or Months 43 and 44)

Topic: True Discipleship and Doing God's Will

Verses: Matthew 7:21-23

Small group theme this month: Knowing Jesus and being his disciple

Your plan this month: Memorize these three verses.

- **Reflection:** What is God's will for your life and for his church in the world? How are you following God's will and joining him in the world and in your neighborhood?

Month 23 (or Months 45 and 46)

Topic: Putting Jesus' Words into Practice
Verses: Matthew 7:24-29
Small group theme this month: Practicing the ethics and ways of the Sermon on the Mount, and being a wise builder
Your plan this month: Memorize these six verses.

- **Reflection:** Have you been a wise builder or a foolish builder? How are you putting Jesus' words and instructions in the Sermon on the Mount into practice through acts of righteousness, peacemaking, love for your enemy, generosity, prayer, humility, faith, forgiveness, reconciliation, discipleship, and more?

Month 24 (or Months 47 and 48)

Topic: Review and Revise
Verses: Matthew 5–7
Small group theme this month: Wrapping up the series: How has the Sermon on the Mount changed our lives, small group, and church and our approaches to social justice, discipleship, and mission?
Your plan this month:

- Spend this month reviewing and revising Matthew 5–7. Practice and consolidate your learning.
- Whether you're memorizing Matthew 5–7 individually or in a group, answer the question in the "Small group theme this month."
- Celebrate your achievement! You've memorized the Sermon on the Mount and sought to put it into practice in your life, your church, and your world!

my personal collection of memory verses

The forty verses we've given you in this book are only a selection of verses worthy of memorization, so you should think beyond the forty verses to a regular, ongoing practice of memorizing Scripture that stretches you into a more mature faith. This appendix allows you to chart your supplemental, aspirational memory verses in each of the five categories.

As you come across new verses in your Bible reading, write them down here, in the appropriate category, and commit to memorizing them in the future.

Bless (Generosity)

_____

_____

_____

_____

_____

Eat (Hospitality)

Listen (Spirit-Led)

Learn (Christlike)

Sent (Missionary)

recommended readings

Here are recommended additional chapters for you to read that will enhance your experience of memorizing these Bible verses. The recommended readings all come from four books by the authors:

Graham Joseph Hill. *Salt, Light, and a City: Conformation—Ecclesiology for the Global Missional Community: Volume 2, Majority World Voices* (Eugene, OR: Cascade, 2020).

Graham Joseph Hill and Grace Ji-Sun Kim. *Healing Our Broken Humanity: Practices for Revitalizing the Church and Renewing the World* (Downers Grove, IL: IVP, 2018).

Michael Frost. *Keep Christianity Weird: Embracing the Discipline of Being Different* (Carol Stream, IL: NavPress, 2018).

Michael Frost. *Surprise the World: The Five Habits of Highly Missional People* (Carol Stream, IL: NavPress, 2016).

Week 1

Topic: Bless

Subtopic: Affirm and Honor Others

Verses: 1 Thessalonians 5:11 and Galatians 3:26-28

Recommended reading: Read chapter 1 of *Surprise the World*. Chapter 1 is titled "Living 'Questionable' Lives."

Week 2

Topic: Bless
Subtopic: Release Finances
Verses: Matthew 6:19-21, 24 and Matthew 6:2-4
Recommended reading: Read chapter 2 of *Surprise the World*. Chapter 2 is titled "A New Set of Habits."

Week 3

Topic: Bless
Subtopic: Exhibit Practical Giving
Verses: 1 John 3:17-18 and 2 Corinthians 8:7
Recommended reading: Read chapter 3 of *Surprise the World*. Chapter 3 is titled "Bless: The First Habit."

Week 4

Topic: Bless
Subtopic: Commit to Prayer
Verses: 1 Timothy 2:1-2 and Jeremiah 29:7
Recommended reading: Read chapter 10 of *Salt, Light, and a City (Volume 2, Majority World Voices)*. Chapter 10 is titled "Conformed to the Image of His Son: On Conformity and Discipleship."

Week 5

Topic: Eat
Subtopic: Welcome Refugees and Immigrants
Verses: Matthew 25:35-36, 40 and Deuteronomy 10:18-19
Recommended reading: Read chapter 4 of *Surprise the World*. Chapter 4 is titled "Eat: The Second Habit."

Week 6

Topic: Eat
Subtopic: Show Hospitality and Welcome
Verses: Luke 14:13-14 and Hebrews 13:2
Recommended reading: Read chapter 6 of *Healing Our Broken Humanity*. Chapter 6 is titled "Reactivate Hospitality."

Week 7

Topic: Eat
Subtopic: Enjoy Table Fellowship
Verses: Luke 7:34-35 and Luke 24:30-31
Recommended reading: Read chapter 13 of *Salt, Light, and a City (Volume 2, Majority World Voices)*. Chapter 13 is titled "Love Your Enemies: On Peacemaking and Suffering."

Week 8

Topic: Eat
Subtopic: Show Justice, Mercy, Compassion
Verses: Zechariah 7:9-10 and James 2:15-17
Recommended reading: Read chapter 6 of *Keep Christianity Weird*. Chapter 6 is titled "Seeing Things Weirdly."

Week 9

Topic: Listen
Subtopic: Repent and Lament
Verses: Acts 3:19-20 and Joel 2:12-13
Recommended reading: Read chapter 2 of *Healing Our Broken Humanity*. Chapter 2 is titled "Renew Lament."

Week 10

Topic: Listen
Subtopic: Be Peacemakers
Verses: Matthew 5:9 and Romans 12:14, 18
Recommended reading: Read chapter 5 of *Surprise the World*. Chapter 5 is titled "Listen: The Third Habit."

Week 11

Topic: Listen
Subtopic: Seek Guidance and Direction
Verses: Psalm 25:4-5 and Proverbs 2:6-9
Recommended reading: Read chapter 12 of *Salt, Light, and a City (Volume 2, Majority World Voices)*. Chapter 12 is titled "Do Justice, Love Mercy, Walk Humbly: On Justice and Activism."

Week 12

Topic: Listen
Subtopic: Be Disciplined and Corrected
Verses: Hebrews 12:7-8, 11 and Revelation 3:19
Recommended reading: Read chapter 3 of *Healing Our Broken Humanity*. Chapter 3 is titled "Repent Together."

Week 13

Topic: Learn
Subtopic: Love God, Neighbors, and Enemies
Verses: Mark 12:30-31 and Matthew 5:43-46
Recommended reading: Read chapter 6 of *Surprise the World*. Chapter 6 is titled "Learn: The Fourth Habit."

Week 14

Topic: Learn
Subtopic: Seek Reconciliation
Verses: 2 Corinthians 5:18 and Colossians 1:19-20
Recommended reading: Read chapter 8 of *Healing Our Broken Humanity*. Chapter 8 is titled "Reconcile Relationships."

Week 15

Topic: Learn
Subtopic: Display Humility and Self-Sacrifice
Verses: Philippians 2:3-4 and Matthew 16:24-25
Recommended reading: Read chapter 11 of *Salt, Light, and a City (Volume 2, Majority World Voices)*. Chapter 11 is titled "He Made Himself Nothing: On Humility and Character."

Week 16

Topic: Learn
Subtopic: Proclaim Freedom and Gospel
Verses: Luke 4:18-19 and Romans 1:16-17
Recommended reading: Read chapter 9 of *Salt, Light, and a City (Volume 2, Majority World Voices)*. Chapter 9 is titled "Of First Importance: On Gospel and Shalom."

Week 17

Topic: Sent
Subtopic: Be a Sent Community
Verses: Matthew 28:18-20 and Acts 1:8
Recommended reading: Read chapter 7 of *Surprise the World*. Chapter 7 is titled "Sent: The Fifth Habit."

Week 18

Topic: Sent
Subtopic: Pursue Justice
Verses: Micah 6:8 and Isaiah 58:6-7
Recommended reading: Read chapter 5 of *Healing Our Broken Humanity*. Chapter 5 is titled "Restore Justice."

Week 19

Topic: Sent
Subtopic: Be Incarnational and Present
Verses: John 20:21 and Amos 5:24
Recommended reading: Read chapter 7 of *Keep Christianity Weird*. Chapter 7 is titled "If We're Not Weird, We're Doing It Wrong."

Week 20

Topic: Sent
Subtopic: Keep Christianity Weird
Verses: 1 Peter 2:9 and Romans 12:1-2
Recommended reading: Read chapter 1 of *Keep Christianity Weird*. Chapter 1 is titled "Here's to the Crazy Ones." Also read chapter 15 of *Salt, Light, and a City (Volume 2, Majority World Voices)*. Chapter 15 is titled "Come, Lord Jesus: Proposals for the *Conformation* of the Church."

notes

INTRODUCTION

1. Kirsten Spruch, "The 14 Best Songs to Sing for Your Ultimate Karaoke Performance," *Baeble Music Blog*, https://www.baeblemusic.com/musicblog/2-26 -2018/the-14-best-songs-to-sing-for-your-ultimate-karaoke-performance.html.
2. Plutarch, *Moralia, Volume I: The Education of Children*, trans. Frank Cole Babbitt, Loeb Classical Library 197 (Cambridge, MA: Harvard University Press, 1927), 13. "Muses" were goddesses who oversaw poetry, music, singing, dancing, comedy, and the like.
3. Brad Leithauser, "Why We Should Memorize," *New Yorker*, January 25, 2013, https://www.newyorker.com/books/page-turner/why-we-should-memorize.
4. Catherine Robson, *Heart Beats: Everyday Life and the Memorized Poem* (Princeton: Princeton University Press, 2012), 96.
5. Rick Warren, quoted in Timothy C. Morgan, "Purpose Driven in Rwanda," *Christianity Today*, October 2005, https://www.christianitytoday.com/ct/2005/ october/17.32/html.
6. Michael Frost, *Surprise the World: The Five Habits of Highly Missional People* (Colorado Springs: NavPress, 2016), xi.
7. Frost, *Surprise the World*, xii.

1 THE BEAUTY OF MEMORIZED TRUTH

1. Becky Baile Crouse, "Warrensburg Church of Brethren Featured in Dunker Punk Podcasts," *Daily-Star Journal* (Warrensburg, MO), May 9, 2019, http://www .dailystarjournal.com/religion/warrensburg-church-of-brethren-featured-in -dunker-punk-podcasts/article_10aa21d4-1fa1-5f10-8dae-62024c0f4deb.html.
2. "The Sermon on the Mount: A Study of Matthew 5–7," Dunker Punks, accessed January 27, 2020, https://dunkerpunks.com/action/sermon-on-the-mount/.
3. Robert Isaac Wilberforce and Samuel Wilberforce, *The Life of William Wilberforce*, (London: John Murray, Albermarle Street, 1839), 5:45.
4. Mary Carruthers and Jan M. Ziolkowski, eds., *The Medieval Craft of Memory: An*

Anthology of Texts and Pictures (Philadelphia, PA: University of Pennsylvania Press, 2002), 3 (italics in the original).

5. Michael Frost, *Surprise the World: The Five Habits of Highly Missional People* (Colorado Springs: NavPress, 2016), 58.

6. Dietrich Bonhoeffer, *Meditating on the Word*, trans. David McI. Gracie (Lanham, MA: Rowman & Littlefield Publishers, 1986, 2000), 117.

7. Richard Clark and Morgan Lee, "John Perkins on the Day He Finally Understood the Bible," *Christianity Today*, May 14, 2018, https://www.christianitytoday.com/ct/2018/may-web-only/john-perkins-on-day-he-finally-understood-bible.html.

8. *Journal and Letters of The Rev. Henry Martyn, B.D.*, ed. S. Wilberforce (London: R. B. Seeley and W. Burnside, 1837), 78.

9. *Journal and Letters of The Rev. Henry Martyn, B.D.*, 78.

10. *Journal and Letters of The Rev. Henry Martyn, B.D.*, 75.

11. Dallas Willard, "Spiritual Formation in Christ for the Whole Life and Whole Person," *Vocatio* 12, no. 2, Spring 2001, 7.

12. Howard Rutledge et al., *In the Presence of Mine Enemies, 1965–1973; A Prisoner of War* (Old Tappan, NJ: Revell, 1973), 34–37. Another downed American serviceman, Bob Shumaker, tried to keep focused by imagining himself building a house for his young wife and the infant son he barely knew. Fellow POW John McCain also discussed this fight against boredom and depression.

13. Brad Leithauser, "Why We Should Memorize," *New Yorker*, January 25, 2013, https://www.newyorker.com/books/page-turner/why-we-should-memorize.

14. Quoted online at: N T. Wright, "Five Texts from Romans to Help You Explore the Whole Bible," *N T. Wright Online*, accessed January 27, 2020, https://ntwrightonline.org/five-texts-romans-help-explore-whole-bible/.

15. Wright, "Five Texts from Romans."

16. N.T. Wright, *Scripture and the Authority of God: How to Read the Bible Today* (San Francisco, CA: HarperCollins, 2013), 130.

17. Wright, *Scripture and the Authority of God*, 130.

18. Wright, *Scripture and the Authority of God*, 133.

19. Wright, *Scripture and the Authority of God*, 134.

2 A BIG, BEAUTIFUL, EXPANSIVE GOSPEL

1. Anthony Schmidt from the Museum of the Bible, quoted in Michel Martin, "Slave Bible from the 1800s Omitted Key Passages That Could Incite Rebellion," *NPR* (Washington, DC), December 9, 2018, https://www.npr.org/2018/12/09/674995075/slave-bible-from-the-1800s-omitted-key-passages-that-could-incite-rebellion.

2. Quoted in Tim Ahrens, "Where You Stand Determines What You See," *Reflections: A Magazine of Theological and Ethical Inquiry from Yale Divinity School*, 2012, https://reflections.yale.edu/article/seize-day-vocation-calling-work/where-you-stand-determines-what-you-see.

3. Griffin Paul Jackson, "The Top Bible Verses of 2018 Don't Come from Jesus or Paul," *Christianity Today*, December 10, 2018, https://www.christianitytoday

.com/news/2018/december/most-popular-bible-verse-2018-youversion-app-bible
-gateway.html.

4. Jackson, "Top Bible Verses of 2018."

5. Quoted in Michael Frost, *The Road to Missional: Journey to the Center of the
Church* (Grand Rapids, MI: Baker, 2011), 33.

6. Frost, *Road to Missional*, 25.

7. N. T. Wright, *Surprised by Hope: Rethinking Heaven, the Resurrection, and the
Mission of the Church* (New York: HarperCollins, 2008), 264–5.

8. David J. Bosch, *Transforming Mission: Paradigm Shifts in Theology of Mission*
(Maryknoll, NY: Orbis, 1991), 430.

9. Tim Foster, *The Suburban Captivity of the Church: Contextualising the Gospel for
Post-Christian Australia* (Melbourne: Acorn, 2014), 23.

10. Foster, *Suburban Captivity*, 22.

11. Daniel Hill, "Funny interaction at breakfast today," Facebook, July 19, 2018,
https://www.facebook.com/search/top/?q=%22daniel%20hill%22%20Funny%20
interaction%20at%20breakfast%20today&epa=SEARCH_BOX.

12. Foster, *Suburban Captivity*, 23.

13. Lisa Sharon Harper, *The Very Good Gospel: How Everything Wrong Can Be Made
Right* (New York, NY: WaterBrook, 2016), 14.

14. Harper, *Very Good Gospel*, 6 (italics in the original).

3 THE ART OF MEMORY

1. Patricia Armstrong, "Bloom's Taxonomy," Vanderbilt University Center for
Teaching, accessed January 28, 2020, https://cft.vanderbilt.edu/guides-sub-pages
/blooms-taxonomy/.

2. Stefanie Weisman, *The Secrets of Top Students: Tips, Tools, and Techniques for Acing
High School and College* (Naperville, IL: Sourcebooks, 2013), 188.

3. Emily Lardner and Gillies Malnarich, "A New Era in Learning-Community
Work: Why the Pedagogy of Intentional Integration Matters," *Change: The
Magazine of Higher Learning*, July–August 2008, https://www.muhlenberg.edu
/media/contentassets/pdf/about/fct/documents/Lardner%20&%20
Malnarich%20%20New%20Era%202008%20Change.pdf.

4. Ed Cooke, "How Narratives Can Aid Memory," *The Guardian* (Sydney)
January 15, 2012, https://www.theguardian.com/lifeandstyle/2012/
jan/15/story-lines-facts.

5. Joshua Foer, *Moonwalking with Einstein: The Art and Science of Remembering
Everything* (New York, NY: Penguin, 2011).

6. Shane Claiborne and Tony Campolo, "Mission and Values: About Us," Red Letter
Christians website, accessed January 28, 2020, https://www.redletterchristians
.org/mission-values/.

7. Quoted in Helen Selsdon, "Helen Keller's Love of Reading," *AFB Blog*, August
27, 2014, https://www.afb.org/blog/entry/helen-kellers-love-reading.

8. Jane Graham, "Andrea Bocelli: 'I Owe My Parents an Awful Lot,'" *The Big Issue*,
January 15, 2019, https://www.bigissue.com/interviews/andrea-bocelli-i
-owe-my-parents-an-awful-lot/.

9. Quoted in Leigh Carriage, "Move Aside Ed Sheeran, 98% of People Can Be Taught to Sing," *The Northern Star* (Surry Hills), May 14, 2018, https://www.northernstar.com.au/news/98-people-can-be-taught-sing/3414355/.

4 THE MEMORY SYSTEM

1. Dallas Willard, "Spiritual Formation in Christ for the Whole Life and Whole Person," *Vocatio* 12, no. 2, Spring 2001, 7.
2. This summary comes from The Navigators' history of the Topical Memory System, available here: https://navhistory.org/2018/11/07/the-topical-memory-system/.
3. Michael Frost, *Surprise the World: The Five Habits of Highly Missional People* (Colorado Springs: NavPress, 2016). We also highly recommend Michael's follow-up book *Keep Christianity Weird: Embracing the Discipline of Being Different* (Colorado Springs: NavPress, 2018) as well as Graham Joseph Hill and Grace Ji-Sun Kim, *Healing Our Broken Humanity: Practices for Revitalizing the Church and Renewing the World* (Downers Grove, IL: IVP, 2018).
4. Frost, *Surprise the World*, x–xi (italics in the original).
5. Phillippa Lally et. al., "How Habits Are Formed: Modelling Habit Formation in the Real World," *European Journal of Social Psychology* 40, no. 6, July 16, 2000, https://doi.org/10.1002/ejsp.674.
6. See, for example: Mandy Oaklander, "The 5 Best Ways to Improve Your Memory," *Time*, September 29, 2015, https://time.com/4042569/how-to-improve-memory/.
7. The Navigators, *Topical Memory System: Hide God's Word in Your Heart* (Colorado Springs, CO: Navpress, 2006), 15–16. Many of these "principles for memorizing Scripture" come from The Navigators' Topical Memory System course workbook.
8. Navigators, *Topical Memory System*, 15.
9. Navigators, *Topical Memory System*, 16.
10. Frost, *Surprise the World*, 22.

5 THE MEMORY VERSES

1. Michael Frost, *Surprise the World: The Five Habits of Highly Missional People* (Colorado Springs: NavPress, 2016), 36.
2. "A Prayer for Generosity," attributed to Ignatius of Loyola.
3. Frost, *Surprise the World*, 46–47.
4. Frost, *Surprise the World*, 68–69.
5. Graham Joseph Hill and Grace Ji-Sun Kim, *Healing Our Broken Humanity: Practices for Revitalizing the Church and Renewing the World* (Downers Grove, IL: IVP, 2018), 29.
6. See the chapter on lament in Hill and Kim, *Healing Our Broken Humanity*. The final sentences are inspired by Psalm 51.
7. Shane Claiborne, Jonathan Wilson-Hartgrove, and Enuma Okoro, *Common Prayer: A Liturgy for Ordinary Radicals* (Grand Rapids, MI: Zondervan, 2016), 382.
8. A prayer written by Graham Joseph Hill. A version of this prayer is published

in chapter 13 of this book: Graham Joseph Hill, *Salt, Light, and a City: Conformation—Ecclesiology for the Global Missional Community: Volume 2, Majority World Voices* (Eugene, OR: Cascade, 2020). Reproduced here with permission.

9. Frost, *Surprise the World*, 72.

10. Brian Zahnd (@BrianZahnd), "The biblical test case for love of God is love of neighbor. The biblical test case for love of neighbor is love of enemy," Twitter, May 29, 2018, 3:26 p.m., https://twitter.com/brianzahnd/status/1001560550004 977664?lang=en.

11. Brenda Salter McNeil, *Roadmap to Reconciliation: Moving Communities into Unity, Wholeness and Justice* (Downers Grove, IL: InterVarsity, 2015), 22.

12. See Natasha Sistrunk Robinson, "Race Matters: Let's Go to the Movies," *A Sista's Journey*, September 12, 2014, https://asistasjourney.com/2014/09/12/ race-matters-lets-go-to-the-movies/; and Natasha Sistrunk Robinson, "Race Matters: Let's Go to the Movies II," *A Sista's Journey*, September 19, 2014, https:// asistasjourney.com/2014/09/19/race-matters-lets-go-to-the-movies-part-ii/. I (Graham) first published this small group activity in the book I wrote with Grace Ji-Sun Kim: Hill and Kim, *Healing Our Broken Humanity*, 151.

13. "A Prayer to #ChangeTheHeart," written by Katherine Rainger.

We recently attended a prayer service that recognized the suffering and courage of Aboriginal and Torres Strait Islander peoples, and which called for truth, justice, and reconciliation. During the service we were moved by the words of Aunty Jean Phillips, as she called for justice and recognition of past and present wrongs against Aboriginal and Torres Strait Islander peoples, but also her modelling of prophetic wisdom and efforts to build bridges. Aunty Jean shows us what it means to seek both peace and justice, love and truth, friendship and reconciliation, and a shared future and solution. In a world where people are constantly shouting over and at each other, we need more Aunty Jean Phillipses, and we need hearts moved by the Holy Spirit toward reconciliation.

This prayer was written by Reverend Katherine Rainger, a nonindigenous Christian, for the #changetheheart prayer service in 2019—a prayer service initiated by Aunty Jean Phillips and supported by Brooke Prentis and the organization Common Grace. The #changetheheart prayer services are a series of events held across the country for truth-telling, prayer, lament, and solidarity on the anniversary of British invasion and colonization. This history and legacy of settler-colonialism is something the land we now call Australia has in common with the United States of America and other countries such as Canada and New Zealand. (Permissions received to include this prayer in our book.)

14. John Dickson, *Humilitas: A Lost Key to Life, Love, and Leadership* (Grand Rapids, MI: Zondervan, 2011), 24.

15. "Prayer of Self-Giving" by Francis of Assisi.

16. See Scot McKnight, *The King Jesus Gospel: The Original Good News Revisited* (Grand Rapids, MI: Zondervan, 2016).

17. Graham Joseph Hill, "Prayer for the Nations." Written for the Micah Australia

Voices for Justice gathering in 2016. Rights retained by Graham Joseph Hill but, nevertheless, used by permission from Micah Australia.

18. Frost, *Surprise the World*, 96–97.
19. David J. Bosch, *Transforming Mission: Paradigm Shifts in Theology of Mission* (Maryknoll, NY: Orbis books, 1991), 519.
20. Adapted from Matthew 28:18-20; Acts 1:8; and Ephesians 6:18-20.
21. Adapted from Micah 6:8; Isaiah 58:6-7; Matthew 6:13; and Romans 12:1-2.
22. Michael Frost, *Incarnate: The Body of Christ in an Age of Disengagement* (Downers Grove, IL: IVP, 2014), from the book's description / back cover.
23. Darrell L. Guder, *The Incarnation and the Church's Witness* (New York, NY: Trinity, 2000), 9 (italics added).
24. "Let Justice Roll Down Like Waters," a prayer by Lauren Lai of Thornleigh Community Baptist Church, Sydney, Australia. Used by permission.
25. Michael Frost, *Keep Christianity Weird: Embracing the Discipline of Being Different* (Colorado Springs: NavPress, 2018), 57.
26. Martin Luther King Jr., *A Gift of Love: Sermons from Strength to Love and Other Preachings* (Boston, MA: Beacon, 2018), 18.
27. Frost, *Keep Christianity Weird*, 50.

6 FREEDOM ON THE OTHER SIDE OF REGULATION
1. George Batista Da Silva, *What They Say: Out of the Screen* (Joinsville: Clube de Autores, 2013), 64.
2. Madeline Bruser, *The Art of Practicing: A Guide to Making Music from the Heart* (New York, NY: Bell Tower, 1997), xiii.
3. Frederick Booth-Tucker, *The Life of Catherine Booth: The Mother of the Salvation Army*, 3rd ed. (London: Salvationist, 1924), 1:15.
4. Booth-Tucker, *Life of Catherine Booth*, 1:52–53.
5. Dan Schawbel, "Jocko Willink: The Relationship between Discipline and Freedom," *Forbes*, October 17, 2017, https://www.forbes.com/sites/danschawbel/2017/10/17/jocko-willink-the-relationship-between-discipline-and-freedom/#2e577a4e6df8.
6. Schawbel, "Jocko Willink."
7. "The Joe Rogan Experience: #958—Jordan Peterson," Podgist Podcast Transcripts, May 9, 2017, https://www.podgist.com/joe-rogan-experience/958-jordan-peterson/index.html.
8. Quoted in Ruth Fishel, *Peace in Our Hearts, Peace in the World: Meditations of Hope and Healing* (New York: Sterling, 2008), 37.

about the authors

MICHAEL FROST is an internationally recognized missiologist and one of the leading voices in the missional-church movement. His books are required reading in colleges and seminaries around the world, and he is much sought after as an international conference speaker. Michael is the founding director of the Tinsley Institute in Sydney, Australia, and the cofounder of the Forge International Mission Training Network. His books include *The Shaping of Things to Come*, *Exiles*, *Incarnate*, *Surprise the World*, and *Keep Christianity Weird*.

GRAHAM JOSEPH HILL is Interim Principal and Director of Research at Stirling Theological College (University of Divinity) in Melbourne, Australia. Graham speaks at conferences, colleges, and seminaries around the world. Graham directs TheGlobalChurchProject.com. His books include *Global Church*; *Healing Our Broken Humanity* (with Grace Ji-Sun Kim); *Salt, Light, and a City*; and *Holding Up Half the Sky*.

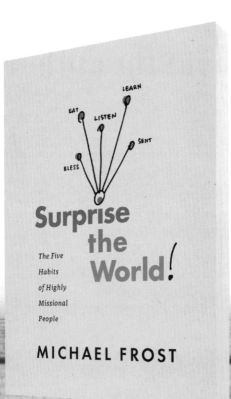

Share your faith
in surprisingly simple ways.

Commit to these simple habits and watch the kingdom of God become tangible. This little book makes it easy to engage in spiritual conversations with anyone. Ideal for personal or group evangelism training.